# The Log-Line

the adventures
of a great sailing
captain

# The Log-Line

the adventures
of a great sailing
captain

*by*

Jessie L. Beattie

*McClelland and Stewart Limited*

0-7710-1166-0

*The Canadian Publishers*
McClelland and Stewart Limited
25 Hollinger Road, Toronto 374

PRINTED AND BOUND IN CANADA

## Acknowledgements

We wish to thank Brown, Son & Ferguson Ltd., Glasgow, for
permission to reprint passage from *The Last of the Windjammers*,
Volume II, by Basil Lubbock; and Mrs. George Bambridge, Macmillan & Company Ltd. and the Macmillan Company of Canada
Ltd. for extract from "The Merchantmen" by Rudyard Kipling.

# An Appreciation

My grateful thanks to Miss Zoe Zimmerman of Hamilton, Ontario, without whose eyes this book could not have been written.

# *Also by Jessie L. Beattie*

*To those*
*who built ships and sailed them*
*dependent upon wind*
*and weather*

# *Foreword*

I introduce the contents of this book with an extract from *The Last of the Windjammers*, Volume II, by Basil Lubbock:

"Amongst the younger commanders, one of the most interesting characters was Captain C. C. Dixon. Small and wiry of build, he was a second Captain Kettle without the pointed beard, and possessed all that intrepid little man's love of adventure.

"The Captain's gig, when Dixon was in command, was constantly in use, for he was a great sportsman in every way, also a naturalist, geologist, and a keen surveyor. If a tropical island happened to be on the course of Dixon's ship, and the weather was favourable, he would swing his Winchester and camera into the gig and, with a crew of four apprentices, would set out on a voyage of exploration. . . . As regards surveying, any little-known island or coastline was always of great interest to the little Captain.

"He had a thousand fathoms of wire on his sounding machine and was always making deep-sea soundings and examining samples of the ocean bed. As an inventor of scientific instruments, he was full of ingenuity. In his saloon, he kept a large chest of assorted wheels, springs, rods, etc., from which he made such instruments as anemometers, wind pressure gauges, deep-sea pressure gauges, etc., and with the help of these his meteorological logs were packed with interesting observations.

He was a keen fisherman, an ornithologist, and an enthusiastic photographer and a cinematographer and, last but not least, a splendid sailor and navigator.

"Captain Dixon commanded the *Arctic Stream* from 1904 to 1912, and the *Elginshire* from 1912 to 1919. The *Arctic Stream* was a fast ship and her passages were always above the average speed even with captains who were not carriers of sail. . . . In 1917 he sailed the *Elginshire* into Durban Harbour without a local chart, without any sailing directions, and without a pilot on board (owing to a misunderstanding with the pilot boat). The little skipper had never been in the port before, and the shipping fraternity of Durban, which is a large and knowledgeable one, made much of him for the exploit.

"As an up-to-date, highly intellectual shipmaster, it would be hard to find Dixon's equal. All who sailed with him became his devoted admirers, and I am not exaggerating when I say that the boys in the half-deck worshipped him as their hero."

A story of Captain Dixon's career at sea, titled *A Million Miles Under Sail*, by John Herries McCulloch, was published by Hurst and Blackett Limited, London, in 1933.

Feeling that many interesting adventures remained to be told, the Captain chose selections from his log and from his many notes. It was my privilege to meet the famous seaman at this time and to be entrusted with the writing of *The Log-Line*, not only from his records but from related stories told to me during many delightful interviews.

That his death occurred before the book's publication was due to a series of misadventures.

A sincere attempt has been made by me to preserve his informative and entertaining style.

During most of Captain Dixon's years in command, he was a Fellow of both the Royal Geographical Society and of the Royal Meteorological Society.

Jessie L. Beattie

# Contents

# The Captain's Introduction

These pages hold simple tales of the sea, of certain ships that sailed and the crews that manned them; also what seafarers saw in ocean and sky, what they encountered on remote islands and forgotten shores.

If these stories measure up to your expectations, we must thank the author who has helped me to put into convincing words a record of what was seen and encountered during thirty-four years of sailing ships.

It will help a lot if you "sign on" with me not as an active member of the crew but just sort of stick by. You really may see even more than I did if you keep your imagination in good working order, for seafarers often miss many wonderful things which are right around them. But in their defence, I must say that landlubbers miss many natural wonders that are all around them, too. This failing of ours was put into beautiful and expressive language by Rudyard Kipling, when he said:

> So dealt God's waters with us
> Beneath the roaring skies.
> So walked His signs and marvels
> All naked to our eyes:
> But we were heading homeward
> With trade to lose or make –

Good Lord, they slipped behind us
In the tailing of our wake!

You will know that the captain of a ship keeps a day-to-day diary or "log"; but you may not understand why the title of this book is called *The Log-Line*, nor why I have divided my story into knots rather than chapters and why I have called the introduction "Stray-Line."

Every sailing ship carries a line of rope. At the very beginning of the line, before you come to the knots, there is a part called "stray-line." The knots aren't the kind you tie and untie but they represent distance on the log-line of the ship and combined with the "log-glass" in an operation known as "heaving the log," they indicate the speed per hour in sailor's miles.

Come, then, sign on with me and let us begin our journey.

Captain C. C. Dixon

# The Log-Line

the adventures
of a great sailing
captain

# The Family Tree

The old world comes,
The new world grows,
And over many lands and seas
Man searches out life's mysteries . . . .

We were sitting by the grate fire in Captain Dixon's study when he began to tell me the story of his adventures at sea. There was a roaring nor'wester outside, giving zest to the leaping flames from the birch log and a flutter to the curtains of the window where the gusts strove to enter through a crevice by the sill.

"I like to look into the flames when I am talking," the Captain said, "although fire is a dread enemy at sea."

He reached for the poker which was on the side next to him and lifted the log slightly, giving fresh impetus to the red tongues already licking it hungrily.

"You had pluck to come out on a night like this," he said, as a spray of sleet hit the window glass. "We're lucky to be on land."

His piercing blue eyes examined me critically. I had not come merely for entertainment. He was sure of that. The publisher who had directed me to him was our mutual friend, and a biography of Dixon published in England some years before had found a Canadian market through his endeavours. But the seaman's most personal and most exciting adventures still remained untold. Time was running out. Although apparently hale and hearty and with a boyish delight in living, the Captain was more than three score years and ten.

He was a small man, his face narrow and lean, his body spare. But his eyes were bright and although there was a determined set to his thin lips, his smile revealed a willingness to communicate. His hair and moustache were snowy white contrasting with the glow of health on his skin – a seaman's skin, ruddy from the whip of sea winds and the touch of salt. He was not a man who had finished with active living; on land, perhaps, for the rest of his life, but still vigorous.

The story of Captain Charles C. Dixon would not be complete without a family tree, especially if valued historically as Canadiana. His twice great grandfather was born in England in 1730, during the reign of George II, a time of unrest and conflict. Charles Stuart, the Pretender, was seeking to take over the English throne.

"It soon became a sort of game, more deadly than rugby," Dixon said. "They chased each other up and down Scotland and England. The cup final was at Culloden Moor. After that, the ardour of both parties cooled and they went home to nurse their wounds and think things over."

Religious intolerance was rampant at that time and when an advocate of peace and decent living in the person of John Wesley preached Methodism, the ancestors of the Captain became his converts.

News from America at this time brought an invitation from Governor Franklin of Nova Scotia to peoples desiring religious freedom. Franklin said they would find this freedom in the new world across the seas. Times were hard in the Isles, especially for the working classes. There was plenty of land in America, and plenty of work, the Governor promised, for those willing to work.

Charles Dixon the first owned a paper mill in Yorkshire and had a large family. Firmly believing that their future lay in America, he sold his mill and set out with his wife and children for Liverpool where the *Duke of York* was about to set sail. After a stormy passage of six weeks when all suffered severe seasickness, the vessel entered Halifax harbour.

18

Enquiry revealed that much land was available for very little at Fort Cumberland. The settlers already there were dissatisfied and desired to leave. It was reported to be a dismal place, but here was a chance for someone determined to be undaunted when faced by the hardships common enough in an undeveloped country.

The Captain's ancestor bought 2,500 acres of land near Sackville.* It was thickly wooded but, with the help of the older children, enough acreage was cleared to allow for growing grain and vegetables. The felled trees were cut into logs and lumber and soon a comfortable enough if primitive home was erected. Their living quarters for some months after arrival had been little more than a one-roomed log shed.

"There was jealousy and friction between the French and the English immigrants at the time," the Captain said, "and after the Boston Tea Party there were war-like movements. The price of goods sky-rocketed too, and the shortage of food was a serious threat to the health of the people. This shortage was worsened by the flocking in of the United Empire Loyalists. Nova Scotia became the byword for poverty, and a common expression was "You look poor enough to belong to Nova Scotia."

But honour was to come to the first Charles Dixon to set foot on Canadian soil. In 1784 the Captain's twice great-grandfather was elected to the first New Brunswick Parliament at a meeting in Parr's Town (later called St. John). That year a son was born, the first of the family to be born in Canada, and the first Charles Dixon to become a seafarer.

At that time shipbuilding was a popular industry in America's port settlements. Ships were built for a number of reasons—for patrolling the coastal waters to frighten away invaders, for acts of piracy to secure booty illegally, for purposes of transportation, and for sale. Charles Dixon built ships for the English market. In 1800 he married Mary Smith, daughter of a minister in Parr's Town. In 1803 the Captain's grandfather was born. The boy grew up among ships and shipbuilders. He watched the

*New Brunswick

19

construction of a craft on which he was to begin his seafaring career although he did not suspect this at the time. This craft when completed was named for the Captain's grandmother—*The Sarah Dixon*. Many good builders assisted in its erection. It was one of the largest ships built in Canada at that time.

*The Sarah Dixon* had a 1468 register and could carry some 2,000 ton of cargo or dead weight. She was 206 feet long and 30.8 feet broad or in beam, and 22.7 feet deep of hold. Years went into the building. She was launched in the early summer of 1856. When finished a few weeks later the ship was sold to a firm in Liverpool. A younger brother of the builder took command. "My father, a boy of fifteen," the Captain explained, "sailed with him as a passenger. He was still too young to 'sign on,' but as he often told me, he had already decided to make seafaring his way of life. *The Sarah Dixon* reached Liverpool safely and by the time all transactions had been completed and she was taken over by her new owners, my father was old enough to be accepted as Boy by the captain of the St. John *Lampedo* which was ready to leave Liverpool—a barque bound for New York. The taste for sea life was in his blood. At New York he transferred to the brig *Mariner* and remained with her for three years."

Three years was then the term of apprenticeship to become an A.B., or Able Seaman. Later the term was four years and some ships demanded six. But boys who had lived in or near seaports and who had learned about ships in their school days, sometimes got by with a shorter period in training at sea than young men from the inlands.

After nine years at sea (in 1871) he came home to Sackville for a long holiday. His parents lived in Sackville but his interest was now centred upon Alicia MacGregor, the attractive young daughter of a British officer. After sailing as mate of the *Annette* from Boston to the West Indies he became skipper of the barque *Cynthia Palmer*. By that time he and Alicia had been married.

Alicia MacGregor had been a school teacher, but her ancestry included Scottish warriors. She loved sea life and her adventurous husband. After several Atlantic voyages they dropped anchor in the port of Windsor, and there Charles Dixon the fourth was born.

"I was nine months old," the Captain said, "when I was first taken to sea. My father was now captain of the *Landseer*, a new barquetine. We were bound for England, the East Indies, the Port of Madras, and from thence to Indo-China. For four full years the *Landseer* traded up and down that coast. Bangkok, Siam, and Melbourne, Australia, were visited before we returned to England at the close of the year 1879.

"Although I was young to be making observations, many experiences encountered impressed themselves upon me and I was later to recall them vividly."

Captain Charles C. Dixon's seafaring career thus begun did not end until 1919. Before he was six years of age he had covered more than 141,000 miles of his record sail of 1,000,000 miles. His adventures on the deep cannot be rivalled in Canadian history.

# My First Voyage

Happenings in the good old *Landseer* were discussed from time to time before me or told directly to me. Also I loved to read over my father's old navigation "Work and Remark" book in which he kept notes different in character from those in the ship's log. Some of his entries dealt with quite personal matters.

It is strange how clear memories of childhood remain even after long eventful years. Many significant occurrences that took place before I was six, both on board and on shore, are among these memories.

One of the earliest voyages which I recall took us to Balasore, India, and another to Sourabaya, Java.

My mother's health was affected unfavourably by the damp moist climate during our stays in India. An Indian nurse known as an *Ayah*, was engaged to keep an eye on me. She travelled with us when we went on short passages across the Bay of Bengal and to Indo-China.

A sister was born to me in Sourabaya, March, 1875, and after that I was left more to the care of the *Ayah*, or with the native boatswain of whom I was very fond. He was with us for several years until we left India to go to Australia and England. This may explain why, at the age of four, I could speak very little English but freely in what I guess you would call "Hindu language." I do not remember much of it now as we did not stay in that trade after I grew up. But they say the subconscious mind never forgets, and I believe this, for often when absorbed in some mechanical operation I find myself repeating words which I certainly do not understand now. Some of the words and phrases which I do remember have become part of the vocabulary of seafarers and soldiers.

My clearest memories of early days are of the terrible Rangoon River while we were at Moulmein, where it rained all the time, and at Bangkok where we were sick with dysentery. My condition became serious and the British doctor gave me up. My father did not accept his opinion as final, however, and hunted up a native doctor. In three days I was well.

In those times we had to beat the *Landseer* up the narrow crooked channels of the river, tacking from side to side and, not to lose an inch, waiting until the jib boom almost touched the mangroves before tacking. It certainly needed nice judgement of speed and momentum or amount of "way." Then we came to part of the river where it was too narrow to work the ship. We now had to anchor. Father went ahead of us with the native boatswain, or sarang, and four coolies, in the ship's small boat or "gig." He took the ship's documents to make his arrival known in order to get the services of a tug to help us up the last part.

Now, although I remained with my mother on the anchored *Landseer*, father told us about how dangerous their trip in the boat had been. Telling the story over and over, I think, relieved him.

They had not been able to go the whole distance in one day, he said, for they were travelling against the current. They had to spend one night in the boat. They had started out in early morning rowing and sailing as opportunity offered. When the sun set they had to anchor, for both river and shore became as black as ink, and the sky heavily overcast. They lit a lantern to hang under the awning that was spread over the boat, but the light brought literally clouds of flying things, from tiny mosquitoes to great moths and bats. These closed in on them until the lantern flame was no longer visible. The light had to be extinguished.

The darkness now covered them from sight of each other. Then came the sound of some heavy body sliding from the banks into the water, perhaps an inquisitive hippopotomus or a crocodile that might be big enough to push the boat over or to bite a piece out of it and thus secure the crew for supper.

Then all was silent for half a minute, my father said. The creature, whatever it was, had moved off, but a new danger threatened: the great tiger made his presence known by the dying shrieks of some animal he was clawing apart.

Feared more than the animals were natives who swam silently and had been known to cut the anchor rope and to tow a boat ashore, there to murder the crew in cold blood. This was a common enough happening in those days, but I do not know of it occurring in Indian waters.

My father and the sarang had old muzzle-loading rifles and the coolies were armed with bayonets from other rifles. The nerves of all were on edge. My father fired a couple of times during the night at dark patches moving past in the current not knowing what they might be. The sound in that black stillness was terrifying. It was instantly followed by the screams of monkeys and birds and a splashing along the shore of the river. The silence that came after was frightening, as if in preparation for something worse to happen.

The coming of dawn, my father said, was a relief beyond words, and that day saw them in Rangoon.

Rangoon is the city of the Great Pagoda. Its dome and spire of pure gold plates was like an enormous fire in the morning sun. Gold was supplied for the plates by natives who brought their rings and other jewellery and cast them into a great furnace where they were melted and then beaten into shape. There is said to be nine English ton, of 2,240 pounds each, valued at some $5,000,000 at the normal valuation of gold, in the dome. It is often spoken of as the *Shwe Dagon*, the central pagoda of the Burmese religion.

Although my father's trip from our ship to Rangoon had been dangerous, I was sorry that I was too young for such adventures, but during his absence I had some of my own. While he was gone, the *Landseer* was in charge of the Mate, Mr. Ben Smith. He was a fine type of Maritimer and later became the Captain of well-known steamers. My father had great trust in him and knew that he would care for our ship as if it were his own, and for all those aboard.

Although the river was wide where we were anchored, we too could hear the noises of the jungle at night. A constant alertness was evident in our crew who realized that thieving natives, if not hostile ones, might try to come aboard in the darkness and take anything or everything movable without making a sound. Our ship was low in the water which made it easier to get on her. The water snakes found this out. They came up the cables and onto the deck, but no harm was done. A very pretty striped fish swam close to the side and Mr. Smith found me almost overboard in an attempt to reach it. He scolded me severely and explained to me that my father would expect me to be a more careful seaman.

I think everyone was mightily relieved to see a small steam launch approaching with my father's boat in tow, a launch which would in turn tow the *Landseer* up to Rangoon.

From Rangoon we began our proper trading and went to many places in India and Indo-China. Among them were Akyab, Chittagong, Vizagapatam and Balasore.

We had our first experience with the unhealthy, unpleasant rainy season in Moulmein. This place has been made famous by Kipling in his "Mandalay" where he refers to "the sludgie, squdgie creeks." That is what they were, with mud, more mud, and still more mud; rain, more rain, and still more rain, for nearly three months.

The dampness was everywhere– in floors and walls, in furniture and clothing, in mattresses and straw mats on which we slept, and, of course, in the bedding. Mildew appeared on everything and food if uncovered moulded in a few hours.

It was necessary to build a fire in the small stove in an attempt to relieve the wetness of the place although the temperature was 90° and sometimes 100°. Hearing of making more heat under such a situation may cause one to feel stifled–but we were often chilly and a fire was welcome.

Dampness is very bad for wooden ships. Wood rotted quickly, in fact about three times as fast as in a temperate climate. Five years of exposure to such conditions was very hard on the *Landseer*, but after leaving India she was fortunate to sail away from the humid atmosphere of the tropics and continued to be seaworthy for many years.

As we went from port to port, with each new cargo, we seemed to accumulate more insect passengers– huge cockroaches and other great and small insects as well as creeping things. Sometimes they appeared in the cargo itself, if of rice, and at other times in the dunnage mats and in the dunnage. The latter consisted of lengths of bamboo which, being hollow, harboured all sorts of insects which came out on the voyage and made the ship their home.

The cockroaches climbed the walls in vast numbers and filled the cracks of partitions until boiling salt water was thrown on them. Then for a day or two we seemed to be rid of them but they soon appeared again in as vast numbers as before.

One evening I made a trip to the pantry for something to eat before going to bed. Holding a candle in one hand, I opened the door of the pantry. As I stepped in, a living cloud made for the candle and extinguished it. In haste I dropped it to wipe off the dozens of winged creatures that had landed on my bare neck and head. They were about two inches long and evil smelling. They did not hesitate to nip one painfully. I ran for Ben Smith who was off duty at the time. He re-lit the candle and came with me. As we brushed the insects out of our way I could hear them scrunching under our feet.

Food was carefully covered. Any left unprotected was nibbled beyond use and had a horrible odour.

Looking back to those days I often wonder how we endured

the hardships which went with sailing in that region. I think of my mother as a heroine. We slept under canopies of mosquito netting but the cockroaches found places to get in. They never attacked my father but my mother's fingertips were often bleeding and painfully sensitive from their nibbling. Sometimes they had a go at me too, I suppose because my flesh was young and tender.

But the cockroaches and flying insects did not worry me like the great spiders. Although the real tarantula is found in Spain, we met with a huge hairy fellow which we called by that name, rightly or not. Its great legs spread out to the size of a large plate. It frightened me by climbing up the outside of the mosquito netting and staring in at me. This spider may be gifted with a high order of intelligence but it displayed a devilish nature as it watched my every move, seeming ready to spring if so much as a toe appeared outside the netting. I learned later that it belonged to the Mygale order, which includes most of the great tropical spiders.

On the floor of the ship, keeping the cockroaches company, were a few centipedes and scorpions, the last more deadly than any other invader of our home. If the scorpion's bite did not kill, it never failed in causing terrible agony. Often I wonder why, for any reason, people voluntarily go to a place where such discomforts and perils must be endured. But the fact remains that they did and do, often in the call of adventure, for monetary gain or in the service of some Christian mission.

A lesson I learned as a boy with so many insects about was the habit of rolling up my clothes and socks at night and bringing them inside the netting curtain with my shoes and slippers. I had no wish to find a spider or scorpion or even a centipede hiding comfortably somewhere in the warmth of my clothing. Again I might not find it until it took a nip out of me, which could have been too late if of a poisonous variety.

A few hundred miles north of Moulmein is the rainiest place in the world. In the mountains of Assam the normal rainfall is 450 inches per year, nearly 38 feet. In the year 1899 the fall was 650 inches, or nearly 54 feet. The rainy season lasts only five months. The rest of the year is dry.

We were in India in 1876 and in a single day the rainfall measured 40 inches, more than the average yearly fall in most parts of Canada. Yet India is such a land of contrasts that some parts are almost rainless, receiving less than 3 inches per year.

On the rainiest day that I remember (with a fall of 40 inches) my father took time to explain to me the significance of nature's behaviour. "Do you know the weight of a deluge like this?" he asked me, going on, "By 10-days' measurement, 2,893,720 tons of water has fallen on one square mile. Suppose something went wrong with the way nature works, such as often goes wrong with man's machinery. Suppose that water condensed all at once. A city would look as if a giant steamroller had gone over it, and if such a weight of water fell on ships at sea they would disappear. But the Mighty Creator planned it differently, and don't forget that the water that falls in rain must first be lifted up by the sun. This is done silently and over large areas. To express the work done in horsepower involves numbers so vast as to be meaningless."

His explanation may not have been as detailed as mine to you but it set me to investigate later and to realize what a master plan directs nature's forces.

Another trial we endured while sailing the *Landseer* in tropical waters was the Brahmin kite. These large dark-coloured birds are very swift of wing. They are scavengers and were protected by the authorities. They seemed to realize this for they were very bold.

When sailing in fine weather and when our ship was in harbour, we ate our meals at a table on deck with a protective awning above it. While we ate the kites would sit in a row on the rail of the *Landseer* or on the edge of the awning. The very second after we had finished and rose from the table they would swoop in and clean up every plate. It was wonderful to see how skilfully they controlled their enormous wings, harming nothing as they flew over the table. But if there was no one to chase them off, they would take all food in the serving dishes as well as the scraps. And if the cook set out something to cool from the galley, it was gone in a half minute.

On this voyage someone gave me an Indian bear cub. It was hardly any larger than an average-sized Teddy Bear, at first, and just about the cutest thing I ever had to play with. We fed it on condensed milk which it sucked through a small roll of muslin. Soon it learned to drink from a dish but only if I knelt beside it with a hand on its furry head. Its behaviour was like that of a puppy at first. It chewed up slippers and shoes if it could find any. Later it preferred those on someone's feet. At first I used to wrestle with it, but before long it was wrestling with me, which was a different matter. It set about chewing not only my shoes and clothes but my feet and hands. This became a favourite pastime for the bear but dangerous for me. Before it had spent a year on the *Landseer*, the bear had grown to twice its size and one day it disappeared.

Although I had suffered a good deal from its behaviour, I was lonesome without it and I plied the crew with questions. I was suspicious that someone had stolen and sold it when we were in port. On the second day without my bear, I would not eat, and was found by my father weeping bitterly. He told me, then, what had been done.

The bear, he said, was now too old to live with human beings, particularly on board a sailing ship. It might have seriously harmed someone in which case it would have had to be destroyed. Mr. Ben Smith, the mate, and my father had taken it in the gig to a nearby shore of its native jungle and released it.

My common sense told me that they had done the right thing but while we remained close enough to the jungle to hear its many sounds I used to listen for my bear's peculiar whine as dusk fell and imagine that I heard it.

# My Second Voyage

During our trading back and forth we called for cargo at a number of small villages. The *Landseer* anchored some distance out, and the cargo was brought to her in canoes. It was exciting to watch the natives manipulate these canoes through the surf.

The bargaining for freight was done by my father who would accompany the merchants to some native hut in the village where the business was settled. Payment was made in rupees, about the size and value of a 50-cent piece. As the freight frequently amounted to several hundred dollars, there were often a number of big bags of this money on board, kept there until we reached a location where there was a banking place.

The native merchants were frequently very wealthy men and appreciated the opportunity of trading. It was their pleasure to give presents–a bolt of native silk, pieces of lace, embroidery, or native jewellery for my mother. For me perhaps small dressed images in costumes representing each class or caste, models of native boats, candies and fruits, and usually some kind of pet–the small bear I loved so much, a parrot, and once a cute little monkey. It was a happy time in the life of a small boy, in spite of spiders and such.

Our cargo became more valuable with freight money and gifts on board. The days of official pirates had passed but there were still sneak-thief natives ready to tackle small unarmed ships.

They would surround them in canoes and climb on board. Also there were the channels and chain plates fixing the rigging to the vessel and forming steps up her side. But the Indian natives did not seriously trouble us. They had the reputation of being kindly and fairly honest.

But when the *Landseer* left Indian waters and went through the Torres Straits en route to Australia we were in real danger. The natives of New Guinea and of many small islands included both pirates and cannibals. Many anxious nights were passed. It was generally calm and we had to drop anchor in case our ship would drift with the current and be shattered on some reef of which there were many.

A very sharp watch was maintained. A small brass cannon was kept loaded, and a dozen old fashioned muskets. That is the only voyage which I remember when I was aware of other weapons on board kept from sight in a locked iron box in my father's cabin–several bayonets and swords.

One very dark night when there was no wind, the water was full of phosphorescence. Long lines of pale green light marked where the current flowed over the edge of a nearby coral reef. The lines resembled the trail of moving canoes. Mr. Ben Smith was on watch. He was sure that they were canoes. He called my father who was lying down. I heard the conversation and followed them to the deck in my night clothes and slippers. Father studied the scene through his night glasses. "You're right," he said to the mate. "But they may not be planning to harm us. We won't shoot to kill but to frighten." Then he saw me. At once he ordered me back to the cabin. As I went I heard the report of the cannon. It was loaded with a mixture of powder, nails and scraps of loose chain. In the light of the explosion they saw that a large dead tree was floating by. The branches looked like the figures of men.

Smiling and relieved my father came to reassure me. My mother held my little sister in her arms and I was crouched beside them, for the report of the cannon in the stillness echoed and re-echoed through the jungle of the neighbouring islands awakening the wild life there. Shrieks and blood-curdling cries were heard and the shrill calling of birds.

At midnight the native boatswain relieved Mr. Smith and the remainder of the night passed uneventfully.

But morning light gave us something to think about. On the deck, close to the starboard side of the main hatch combing, lay a native knife. It had apparently been thrown for it had marked the combing before falling to the deck. In the main rail abreast the rigging was another, still in position.

"We did right to fire," my father said. "There may have been a canoe under the stern of the vessel. Certainly we were going to be attacked." He praised Mr. Smith for his alertness. But for the quick action of the mate I might have been converted into "long pig" and served with curry to some cannibal chief.

When making trips across the Bay of Bengal, we were quite often becalmed, especially during the south-west monsoons which occurred in the rainy seasons.

On such occasions when there was only a gentle breeze and the *Landseer* was moving at about two knots, I enjoyed myself the most for then the water was as clear as glass. The fish that were of many kinds could be plainly seen.

The *Landseer* was an older type vessel with a huge rudder-trunk or tube, built of wood. The rudder-head led through this from the main part of the rudder to where the tiller and the steering tackle were fixed. The trunk, of course, had to be very much larger than the rudder-stock or head in order that the latter could be moved from side to side. Down the space between these two I could see into the deep. I could watch whatever might come swimming around the rudder. Also, I could fish. Sometimes I fished all day long. When the rudder was "hard over," the open space between it and the trunk was wide enough for me to fall through. This worried my mother and I was required to wear a big pith helmet.

One species of fish commonly seen was called "Old Wives"*

* Possibly a type of ale-wife

by the seamen because it moved very slowly with a sort of shuffle. I asked Mr. Smith what this fish would take as bait. He said that they couldn't be caught with a hook. They had to be speared with a barbed and pronged fork. This I was not big enough to handle I knew, but how very much I wanted to catch one, I also knew.

I was not discouraged by my good friend, the mate. My line was long enough to reach them but my hook was small. However, I baited it with a piece of meat and dropped it down but they did not even look at it. I watched for a long time, my line still dangling, and I noticed that they were taking barnacles from the ship's side.

I told Mr. Smith when he came to have a look. We were great friends, and when he was off watch and visiting in the cabin with us, I called him "uncle."

Mr. Smith ordered one of the crew, a native, to pick a few barnacles for me. I was excited and certain of success, but the mate was discouraging. "They won't take a hook," he said again.

"They like barnacles. They'll take this one," I declared as I baited it carefully.

They did seem tempted a bit. They sidled up with their slow easy motion and one even took a nip at the barnacle but swam away unharmed.

They were not large—about a foot long and four or five inches wide. The mouth was small.

"My hook is too big," I thought. I tried a tiny one, affixing the barnacle with difficulty. It actually disappeared into an "Old Wife's" mouth.

"I've got one," I shouted, giving the line a quick jerk. But I spoke too soon. When I pulled up the line, both bait and hook were gone.

Mr. Smith came over smiling. "I'm going to try again," I said. "May I please have another hook—a bigger one?"

He brought one to me. "But you won't catch an Old Wife," he said.

I didn't answer except to thank him. I was of a different

opinion. I attached the hook and chose the biggest barnacle to bait it, leaving the barnacle well over the tip. Again the fish came sidling up, gave it a nudge and swam away. But in a half minute it was back again. As it sort of leaned its head over the barnacle, I did not wait for a nibble. I gave a sharp jerk and had it. I shouted my luck to everyone as I pulled my fish up the 12 feet of rudder-trunk to the deck. Again I called excitedly for the mate. He is almost as pleased as I am, was my thought as he unhooked my catch.

"Well done," he said. "That's the first one I ever saw taken with a hook. And did you know they're good to eat? Give it to the steward and he'll cook it for your supper."

But before going to the steward with my prize, I enlisted the praise of my father and mother, and then took time to examine the fish. It had teeth like a pair of wire-cutters, strong enough to remove barnacles and to crush them. The poor thing kept grunting like a little pig. I felt sorry for it and asked my father if I should let it go in the sea, but he assured me that it would only float away to die or, in its wounded state, be eaten by some other sea creature.

I took it to the steward then, and my parents and Mr. Smith, as well as myself, had a taste of it for the evening meal.

One day, some weeks later, when on my watch-tower, I spied a beautiful young dolphin. It was swimming close to the rudder with its eye on a tiny fish which was keeping very near to the ship's side for safety. They moved out of my range, and I leaned down to watch them. As I did so, I felt a painful crushing about my head and pulled up to free myself. When I could not do so, I struggled to get free of my helmet but failed in this also. I cried out for help and my father and the mate came running. My father grabbed the wheel from the paralyzed native helmsman who, I suppose, thought he had killed me. Once the wheel was put over, I was released.

My father found me unhurt but I was marched off to the cabin where my mother warned me that unless I was more careful, my favourite pastime would be stopped. I returned to the deck to see my helmet which had fallen down the rudder-trunk when I was released, floating slowly astern like a tiny tub-shaped boat. As I watched, I wished that I could sail away like Wynken, Blynken, and Nod, about whom my mother had been reading to me only that morning. I felt deeply ashamed and temporarily friendless.

KNOT FOUR

# Storms and St. Elmo's Fire

One well-remembered voyage began when I was eight. My father was taking a cargo of coal from Liverpool, England, to Valparaiso, Chile.

The ship was the s.s. *Vaughan*, a 900-ton barque. It was a craft worthy of praise for it came through some of the roughest weather which I recall encountering at sea. The way in which my father met and dealt with danger helped me to meet later perils when I became a skipper myself. Example impresses a child more than words.

First of all we ran into a fierce tempest in the Irish Sea. The second test of our ship's strength and of the wisdom and endurance of its master came as we approached the Cape at the extreme tip of South America.

In the Irish Sea we sailed into a wicked south-east wind which forced our ship to drift dangerously toward shore. The water turned a yellowish colour and the waves crashed onto the deck. It was impossible to move forward. My father ordered the anchors dropped.

My mother and I had been on deck but my father sent us below. It was possible to hear there better than above, the shouted orders which cut through the blast. "They're taking down the sails," my mother explained. "Soon only the sticks will be left."

My mother opened a book of my favourite animal stories and began to read to me. Her voice was like an intermittent thread of melody running through a crescendo that repeated itself many times. She knew that I was only behaving politely in respect for her efforts to distract my attention from what was taking place above, and finally she laid the book aside. Trying to smile, she said, "Your father likes to command a ship in a storm. He'll be tired but happy when it's over."

Her voice conveyed her confidence that we were quite safe and I asked, "May I go up and help him?"

Her answer respected my impulse as she looked deep into my eyes. "He is in command and he ordered us to come here. He knows where to find us."

"When I'm captain of a ship, I will expect everybody to obey me, too," I said.

My father remained on deck all that day. He usually ate the noonday meal with us in the cabin but it was almost sunset before he came in. He was dripping wet and his face was blistered from contact with the battering water which was more hurtful because filled with sand.

Without speaking he lay down on a leather couch and closed his eyes. My mother put a finger to her lips, but although we didn't speak to him, we could tell that he was listening–listening to the groans of the straining ship and the shouts of the Mate giving orders.

Then came a terrible lurch and a bounce upward as if the waters were throwing the barque out of them into the towering heavens. Father leaped to his feet and was gone.

My mother knew what the motion had indicated. "The cable must have snapped . . . we're dipping. But everything will be fixed up," she hurried to add, "and maybe the storm will grow weaker now that the sun has gone down." But she took my hand and went toward the companionway. I felt sure that we were in real danger, now, but of course we would come through alright. I could remember other storms but none quite so violent as this one. However, with my father out there, somewhere, his voice still strong above the pound of the waves, all would be well in time.

Later in life, in recalling that storm which lasted four days and four nights, I knew that only master seamanship saved us.

One emergency followed another. Each had to be met with quick sound judgement and with courage. It was a tense moment when, on the third day, my father came below and wrote some words on a slip of paper. He put the paper into a cask weighted at one end and flagged at the other; then he threw the cask overboard into the raging sea. My mother explained that he hoped the cask would be carried to shore; that this was a seaman's way of asking for help.

That was midday. The remnant of rope salvaged from the snapped cable had been attached to the one remaining, in order to strengthen it so the ship's bow would not be tipped as deeply under water. She had partly righted herself and if the lengthened cable lasted out until help came, all would be well.

For the rest of that day and the following night, my father did not come below. Fully dressed, my mother and I lay sleepless. It was dawn when my father appeared at the cabin door. He said one word, "Pray," and disappeared. My mother knelt and drew me with her.

About noon a lifeboat appeared. The storm had noticeably abated by then.

"Are you ready to abandon ship?" someone in the boat shouted.

"No," roared my father. "I asked for a tug."

Daylight was fading when a tug finally reached us and towed us to shore. I was allowed on deck to watch this operation and my mother came with me. As we left the ship, I noticed that my father, who was with us, was holding fast to the arm of a crewman.

When we stood at last on land, he said quietly, "I can't see."

The lashing waters of the storm, full of sand, had blinded him, and the s.s. *Vaughan* was cleaner than I had ever seen her, by the same harsh treatment that had affected my father's sight. He was taken immediately to a hospital where for some days his vision was despaired of, but by the time our good ship was repaired and ready for sailing again, so was her captain.

Extensive repairs were needed for we had lost our masts with tons of yards as well as rigging that had been cut away, and much gear. However, the s.s. *Vaughan* was as good as new when we set off a second time for South America.

But we were not finished with bad weather. Ships rounding Cape Horn are always prepared for difficulties. We certainly had them. Just as we came around, we met a storm of such fury, accompanied by such high seas that our good ship was caused to lurch seriously. Our cargo of coal shifted, causing a lop-sided position, with our lee rail submerged under almost 6 feet of boiling water, boiling in appearance with spray like steam. It was after dark. We were on the verge of going right over. To prevent this the lower topsails were cut, then the mizzens, but before the sail would come down, the sheet had to be cut also. This meant searching for the part hidden under water on the lee side. My father depended on the skill and daring of our first mate, Mr. Ben Smith, for this job. He used a sheath knife fastened to the end of a boat hook to find the rope and with the knife completed the job. The great canvas flew away like an immense bird. The s.s. *Vaughan* didn't level, however, until we got into the lee of a huge island just off the Cape with straits called Le Maitre separating it from the mainland. This took all night. In the morning, in calmer water, the crew set about shovelling the shifted cargo into proper balance.

The sea had become my home by this time and I accepted all emergencies as part of an exciting adventure, not fearing, because was not my own wise father in command? It was thrilling and marvelling. The rest of our voyage was reasonably uneventful except that crossing the Equator for the first time worried me. I had been told that the heat would scorch a man's skin until it curled up in black crinkles. I was disappointed to find the weather only slightly hotter than I had experienced during the hottest days of summer in Canada. I deliberately exposed the upper part of my body but except for a mild sunburn, nothing happened.

I was to cross the Equator numerous times later in life and never with any serious distress as to temperature. Many stories of the sea are highly coloured to astonish and excite the reader. I find sticking to the truth exciting enough.

The voyage homeward was free from dangerous storms and I was sorry when we reached England again. I was disappointed when I learned that instead of being taught by my mother, as I had been, arrangements had been made to place me in a boys' school there. I became a landlubber in habit but not in spirit. The education which I received was valuable to me in later years, however, I admit. But how happy I was when I stood again by my father, a year later, in the bow of the *Marabout*, of St. John, New Brunswick, as it set sail for Manila! My education on land was only intermittent until 1889 when I turned eagerly to the business of becoming another member of the Dixon line of seafarers.

The most weird display of nature at sea is St. Elmo's Fire.

I was only ten years old when it made a very deep impression upon me.

My father was Captain of the *Marabout*. This ship was of 1498 tonnage register. She was built at St. John, New Brunswick, in 1882, and did not complete her career until five years after World War I.

We were bound for the Philippine Islands. We set sail from New York and had just completed a few day's "running our easting down" and had turned north to the Straits of Sunda. Here we found warmer, finer weather and one of nature's greatest spectacles – the eruption of Krakatoa. Its awful work had just been completed.

Krakatoa was an island with Java on one side and Sumatra on the other. The sea in that region was full of pumice stone and the air almost choked us it was so thick with dust. The sun was invisible. Darkness lasted for three days and nights. The island had vanished in an explosion under the sea which had blown it to atoms. Krakatoa had covered 18 square miles and had a height of from 200 to 1400 feet above sea level. The vibration from the volcano's eruption is said to have passed and returned at least three times around the world, and the waves of great height which it originated were felt by ships in the English Channel more than a thousand miles away. Many ships had been in the area and they were never seen again. They were either engulfed or blown to bits.

We had just missed a like fate.

The *Marabout* was the first full-rigged ship I had been in and I never tired of gazing in wonder at the great yards and the masts, so different to those of our little *Landseer*.

As we left the Straits of Sunda behind, it was two bells in the second dog-watch. The sky was still overcast with heavy dark clouds. The wind was from the north-west and we were streaking northward toward the Trade Winds and better weather. We were sailing at top speed.

The mate was at the wheel and I was close beside him, glad to be near someone when I looked at the threatening sky. We were now beyond the unnatural darkness of the Krakatoa disaster but an oncoming storm was producing a like effect—it was growing darker every minute and very soon it was as pitch black as "the inside of a squaw's pocket." Now the sea took on a strange brilliance produced by phosphorescence. Soon the waves resembled great green flames.

Then came the squall—with a ferocious wind and sheets of rain. Indeed the rain was so heavy that one was actually in danger of smothering from the quantity of water lashing one's face.

The ship heeled suddenly to the wind and the lee-rail disappeared below the mountainous green waves.

Now there was a wild cracking above as two of the top gallants were ripped apart. The sound of splitting canvas was like that of battering machine guns. The tattered ribbons could be plainly seen touched with the same weird light as that upon the sea. What appeared to be flames ran along the lee-side of the deck seeming to lick up everything. They mounted the ropes and rigging. It was a terrifying sight.

Then suddenly the wind and the rain stopped. The good old *Marabout* came upright with a jerk when the pressure was removed. Almost at the same instant the phosphorescent light disappeared. We were in inky blackness again and in silence except for the noise of the water pouring out of the scuppers, and the waves which were still coming over the bow. The effect was as if one were suddenly thrust into a sound-proof room. Then on the trucks of the three masts appeared a golden glow like a halo. The haloes became brighter and larger; then the same golden glow appeared on the Royal yard-arms, on the top gallant, and a golden ribbon crept down the backstays. Soon the glow was on all the yard extremities and down the backstays to the same level.

I watched this phenomenon scarcely breathing as it appeared on the head of a man standing in the rigging. He was knotting some broken ropes. The brilliant halo cast its light over the man's face making it look like the face of a corpse.

Then came a blinding flash of lightning followed by earsplitting thunder, sheets of hail and a roaring wind.

When we recovered from a condition which had temporarily blinded us, the phenomenon had vanished, the "line-squall" had passed, and a gale from the south was upon us in the inky darkness. Above the sound of wind and waves the shouts of the crew in action were heard as the mate roared out his orders.

In the dim light from the binnacle I could see my father assisting the helmsman to control the speeding ship. She steadied and soon we were safely on our course toward the Trade Winds and the summer seas.

Since that time I have seen several displays of St. Elmo's Fire, as it is called, but never one approaching in brilliance that which took place on the *Marabout*'s sail to Manila.

All hands were on deck during this dreadful storm and it was a tired but thankful crew that returned to regular watches. As the sea grew calm we dropped anchor. Hot coffee from the galley refreshed everyone. The men had little to say as they drank heartily and thankfully. It had been a close call but no lives had been lost, nobody washed overboard, and our good ship was all in one piece.

I was to experience many storms in many parts of the world for I would have a seafaring career too, when I became old enough.

After attending school in England I rejoined my parents in 1889. My father was now Captain of a famous ship, the *Erin's Isle*, and I became her deck-boy. She was built in Nova Scotia but her home port was Liverpool.

The *Erin's Isle* was a full-rigged ship. She was beautifully constructed with an outside planking and an inside flooring a foot in thickness. She was built for beauty and strength, but not for speed.

I was proud to be one of her crew, though mine was a humble position when we sailed from New York to Liverpool and on to Rio de Janeiro. We were carrying coal.

When we left Liverpool I was close to sixteen. The night before we put out, my father called me aside. "You've had quite a few years of sea life for a boy your age," he said. "But until now you've been under my direct command. You've never given me reason to be ashamed that you are my son and I feel confident that you never will. But as from now you will be one of the crew and under the orders of the ship's officers. You will live with the ordinary seamen and take duty with the Mate in the port watch. You are now a man."

After that I received no special consideration. Indeed, my father all but ignored me, leaving me to find for myself a place among the members of the ship's crew.

# A Day on Board

One of the most important things in the world, not only on board ship but everywhere, is time. Time to get up, time to eat, time to sleep, and time to carry on our various duties.

Time at sea is even more important than on land because if we lose track of it, there is no means of finding it again, until sailors get to port. At least that was true in the days of sailing ships; and when at last we were able to tell in which meridian we were, it was possibly too late to take advantage of our length of day.

Suppose you were driving along a lonely country road. As you passed by someone walking, perhaps a camper, you stopped and asked, "Where am I?" And he replied, "I don't know what time it is in London so I can't tell you." Wouldn't you think that an odd reply? And yet, on a ship, that is the information needed to tell the time on board.

A crew is divided into watches so that a certain number of men are on duty night and day to navigate and steer and do the general work on shipboard. There are some, of course, who do only day work and sleep at night, such as the cook, the steward and his helpers, carpenter, sailmaker, blacksmith, and others. But these men have no part in the actual sailing of the ship.

During my life at sea there were two common systems of watches. The two-watch system, and the three-watch system.

There were others in use but I knew little of them. The two-watch system was that used on sailing ships and on all cargo steamers. On passenger liners, the three-watch system was used instead and has been adopted by cargo boats in recent years.

On sailing ships during my time, the seamen were divided into Starboard Watch and Port Watch. The Second Mate was in charge of Starboard Watch and the Mate of Port Watch. Whichever officer was on duty took over the operation of the ship with his men. At the end of four hours he was relieved by the other officer and his men. Every four hours the Watch was changed, except in the period between 4 p.m. and 8 p.m. which was divided into two Watches known as the First and Second Dog Watch. I shall explain the purpose of this arrangement later.

The time to "change the Watch" had to be announced in some way and this was done by striking a bell. One bell was suspended near the wheel or from a structure on the poop, perhaps from the top of the wheel box or from a guard-rail across the poop and skylight. The other bell was fixed at the bow of the ship.

The ship's clock was in the cabin or saloon where we ate our meals, and was placed where it could be seen from the skylight. In each Watch, one of the boys looked after the time.

Let us follow the clock from 12 a.m. of one day to 12 a.m. of the next day, and see what happens. The Watch has just been changed and the Starboard Watch and Second Mate have come on duty to take charge of the deck. At 12:30 p.m. the boy strikes the bell. At 1 p.m. he strikes twice in quick succession and that is called Two Bells. For each half hour from 12 noon or the beginning of the Watch, one bell stroke is added.

At 4 p.m. the Watch is changed and the Mate and Port Watch come on duty. Now the bells start all over again. Each time that Eight Bells is reached, the Watch is changed: at noon, at 4 p.m., 8 p.m., midnight, 4 a.m., 8 a.m., and at noon again. There are six 4-hour Watches in each full day.

By this we see that two groups of people and six 4-hour

periods would bring about the same group on the same hours of duty, day after day, which would mean that if the Mate and his men came on at 8 p.m., until midnight, they would be on again at 4 a.m., giving them only a 4-hour sleep during each night while the other Watch would have 8-hours sleep each night. This would have been unfair. Therefore the Dog Watches were introduced. The period from 4 p.m. to 8 p.m. was divided into two 2-hour Watches to overcome this. By this plan, the Watches changed places—one night the Mate and his men had an 8-hour sleep, and the next night, the Second Mate and his men had likewise.

Of course, in stormy weather both Watches were often needed, and the Watch off duty might be called out too. Perhaps the job which had to be done would take an hour or more and they would just get to sleep again when it would be time to change the Watch.

In calm weather they had regular hours but there was little of what is known as spare time, and sleep was cut to a minimum. Let us follow the crew for a day on board and see what their duties are.

At 4 a.m., the Watch on duty is assembled at the front of the poop. When all are there, one calls to the officer, "All aft, sir." If the Mate is the one in charge, he looks the group over, counting them to see that all are there. If satisfied, he repeats, "All aft, Mister," to the Second Mate who has been in charge of the ship up to that hour.

If there is no work to be done, he says, "Relieve the wheel and look-out —that'll do the Watch." Immediately he sends one man to the wheel to relieve the one who has been steering the ship and another to the look-out in the forward part of the ship to do the same.

The Mate is told by the Second Mate what course the ship has been steering and the course it is to steer, and any other order which the latter may have received from the Captain.

In some sailing ships and all steamers there is a Night Order

Book in which the Captain has written directions as to the course to steer and when he is to be called. But in a ship without an order book, the Second Mate says to the Mate, "Course is WNW–the Captain wants to be called if the wind hauls ahead, and at 6 a.m. in any case. Everything is on her–(that is, she has her sails all on)–And that bank of cloud (or weather-bow), isn't pretty. I'm off."

The Mate repeats the course WNW and says, "O.K."

At 4:30 the boy strikes the bell and goes to call the cook for it is time to make the fire in the galley. At 5 o'clock, or Two Bells, the steward is called. By this time the morning coffee is ready for the men. Somebody relieves the man at the wheel, another the one in the look-out, until they have their share, which is served with a couple of slices of bread or hard biscuits. The steward serves the breakfast to the boys and takes it to the Mate on the poop, for the Mate cannot come down. An officer on duty must not leave his post unless relieved by another, and no sailor is allowed to sit down while on duty. But in a sailing ship, this rule is sometimes relaxed in fine weather; on a steamer it is never relaxed.

The morning is fine so the Mate enjoys his coffee and biscuits as he sits at ease on the rail or on the corner of the skylight. We are in the north-east Trade Wind region of the North Atlantic bound for Liverpool, England. It is May, and summer in the northern hemisphere. We are in latitude 18 degrees north.

It is already good daylight by the time the Mate has finished his coffee. He goes to the front of the poop and yells for the deck boy. The boy comes running and takes a hasty look at the clock as he does so.

The Mate says, "What's the time, son?"

The boy replies, "Twenty after five."

"Make it three bells. Come on Boy, we've got lots to do. Go and call those two loafers, the carpenter and the sailmaker. And is the Boatswain out? They'd sleep all day if you'd let them. When you come aft bring the broom, tell the Boatswain

17

I'm waiting to see him. Now git and don't stay in the pantry."
He gives him his coffee mug to return there, as he speaks.

To the Boatswain as he comes aft, the Mate says, "Get those
men along and get her washed down."

The process of washing the deck was carried out until Six
Bells or 7 a.m. Then brooms and buckets were put away.

Now the Boatswain comes to the Mate again and is given
orders as to what work is to be started for the day. If there
are special jobs to be assigned to special men, he orders them
also. This morning we are painting the ship. The yards and
masts have been painted some weeks ago while we were in the
south-east Trades in the South Atlantic. Some of the deck fittings
have had a first coat also. Today we are to paint the bulwarks,
the houses and the remainder of the fittings. This work is
finished up as general routine.

In order to give the Watch coming on duty at 8 a.m. a few
minutes extra to get up, dress, and breakfast, seven bells is
struck at 7:20 instead of at 7:30 a.m. (The officer in charge
of this Watch was the Second Mate. He was not called until
7:45 a.m. The boy looking after the time, struck the bell once,
and went to wake him.)

"One bell, Mister," he says.

"What's the weather?"

"Fine, Mister. Fine."

Had the boy reported rainy weather the Second Mate would
have donned oilskin and sea boots.

Although the officer on Watch was relieved at 8 o'clock, after
breakfasting in the cabin with the Captain, he had still to relieve
the one who had just taken over his duties until he, too, had
breakfasted.

It is 10 a.m. before he is finished with all work and is free
to lie down to rest until 11:30 a.m. Although his Watch does
not begin until 12 noon he has to be on hand earlier to assist
the Captain in taking sun observations with a sextant, by means
of which the position of the ship is determined.

48

At Seven Bells, or 11:30 a.m., the sleeping Watch is called for dinner, to be ready for duty at Eight Bells or 12 noon; then those relieved have their meal and turn in.

Either the Mate or the Second Mate is on Watch every minute, for a ship is never left without an officer on deck, night or day. But in the afternoon, the officer has the Boatswain to help him in his Watch in looking after the work of the ship, which leaves the officer free to make an inspection.

Now, at 4 p.m. the first Dog Watch begins. The Watch have their tea, and half an hour later start to clear the deck of things with which they have been working. The boy is sent aloft to overhaul and stop the bunt-line ropes that would chafe the sail if left taut.

That day, the things to be put away were paint pails and brushes. The deck was clean and did not need sweeping, which was fortunate for the dust might have settled into the paint.

The Watch is changed again at 6 p.m. but it is now after working hours, so only one man has work to do–the one whose turn it is to take the wheel. This is the Watch so often written about in sea stories–a time when the crew may relax and sit around on the main hatch, yarning and smoking. If in a part of the world and during a season when the days are long, and the sun still up, they sometimes work for themselves, repairing clothing or carrying on some hobby. In fine warm weather, if the days were short and it darkened early, some sat in the forecastle (fo'c'sle) where there was an oil lamp, to work and to read, or lay resting on their bunks.

The second Dog Watch, in fine weather, was the only time in the 24 hours of the day in which all of the men in the fo'c'sle could get together. At other times the Watch coming on duty went right on deck while the others went below.

Many and many a time when I was quite young and sailing with my father and mother, about the time darkness fell, I would sneak forward to the hatch to listen to the stories of the men. I was forbidden to do this because my father thought that their conversation might not be suitable for a small boy to hear; but I did it secretly. The men paid no attention to me. I think they resented my being there, probably fearing that I might hear murmurs of discontent and report them to their Captain. Perhaps my father knew their feelings and did not want to annoy them, as well as wanting to protect me. Anyway, I was found by him on several occasions and severely punished for my disobedience.

I remember one occasion which almost cured me. I had crept forward, and was thrilled to find the sailors telling the story of a haunted ship. I listened with ever-increasing interest, creeping nearer and nearer as the tale developed in horror and detail. When it was ended, I was almost too scared to move, let alone go along the deck to the cabin. Then as the bell struck at a quarter to eight, the men got up off the hatch and moved forward, leaving me alone.

As I stood trembling and trying to get courage to go aft, I thought I saw the ghost which they had been describing, walking along the deck towards me. Screaming, I fled from it. I tripped over a loose rope and shrieked, thinking that it had overtaken me.

My father and mother rushed out of the cabin to see what was happening. When I could get my breath, I tried to explain. My mother put an arm around me then, but my father said sternly, "Perhaps you won't disobey me after this."

The Dog Watch might be called the romantic watch of the day. Long ago, it was in this Watch that evil plots were hatched by discontented members of the ship's crew. The historic mutinies of the eighteenth century took place at 7 p.m., or Six Bells in the Second Dog Watch. From that time on, this Watch was never struck in British sailing ships. Instead of 6:30 p.m., being Five Bells, and 7 p.m. being Six Bells, as in other Watches, after Four Bells was struck at 6 p.m., they started all over again. Then 6:30 p.m. became One Bell and 7 p.m. Two Bells. But 8 p.m., as was the former custom, was resumed by striking Eight Bells. After that time it went on in the usual way.

After Eight Bells, the Second Mate comes on duty and the Starboard Watch begins, which means that the Mate and the Port Watch are to have 8 hours of sleep that night. They will come on at 4 a.m. at which time our 24 hours on board ship will be complete, bringing a new day and a repetition of what I have told you.

# Birds at Sea

A great many of the common land birds are found far at sea, sometimes blown out by gales while migrating from the coast which they have been following. But there are numerous birds which are ocean birds and these I know more about, for every large body of water in the world has its creatures of the air as well as those of the deep.

Probably the commonest and most often caught is the booby. I don't know how it got the rather uncomplimentary name, unless because it allows the frigate bird to steal its food. As the booby goes home from a good day's fishing, its stomach well-filled, it is sighted by this enemy which swoops down as if to strike it. The swooping continues until the booby sees he cannot get away and decides to give up part of his hard-earned and as yet undigested supper. This he does and in a flash the frigate bird has dived and neatly caught the falling fish in his long beak, before it can reach the surface of the water. If he decides that is all the booby has to give him, well and good, he flies off, but if he thinks it is holding out against him, he will follow it until he gets what he wants.

The booby is a variety of the Gannet family. He is about the size of a gull but with a longer and slimmer body, with slim straight pointed wings. These are brown and the breast is white. His beak is yellow and pointed. Although he can land and rise from the water, he does not seem to like doing it.

Instead, he alights on any yard of a ship, perching there at dusk. Sometimes we located the bird's perch before it was quite dark and climbed up afterwards to catch him. This was easy to do if one was careful to avoid the pecks of his sharply tapered beak. We caught this bird for examination, not to kill, for he was useless as meat and it was not my habit to destroy life unless for some worthwhile purpose.

The most restless bird I ever caught at sea was the stormy petrel or Mother Carey's chicken. This is the frequenter of most oceans and is common in many localities crossed by passenger vessels. People speak of it as the little black dancer of the waves, and this is a good name for it. There are several species but the most common has a white band on the tail and short broad wings like a butterfly, whose flight it seems to copy.

Although it weighs a mere ounce and a half or so and is literally nothing but feathers, it has a wing spread of over a foot. I think of all birds on the wing the petrel is supreme as to endurance. For a whole day and indeed for days on end, it can keep up its water dance. Nor does a violent tempest worry it. In all my thirty-four years at sea, I have not seen the petrel at rest on the surface, with wings folded, more than a dozen times, and those were during a perfect calm. When it sleeps and where, we do not know. There is a legend which tells of a wonderful ship, a perfect ship, which has a bell large enough for the stormy petrel to house within and to rest as long as it desires. But on this vessel nothing is as sailors have known it, for the ship owner and the captain work while the sailors enjoy themselves in idleness and luxury. And this is the only place that the most restless little bird of the ocean is found resting.

The frigate bird which lives on the fish catch of other birds and floating refuse, sails about like a huge kite, some 2,000 to 3,000 feet above the water. I have never seen it at rest either. It is a black colour and has exposed flesh on its head and neck like most vultures. It measures about six feet from wing tip to wing tip. Its wings are tapered and it has a swallow tail.

Being an excellent scavenger, it is protected by the Government and enjoys a life comparatively free from attack. This is not a beautiful bird when close at hand but its dark shape against a deep blue sky on a clear morning is something to remember.

The largest flying bird of the world is the wandering albatross which some people think no longer exists. This is not true, as I have seen many of them and they may be found anywhere south of the tropics, but today few vessels pass through the regions where they can be seen.

Long ago, sailors believed that if anyone on board was responsible for the killing of one of these huge birds, bad luck would follow the ship thereafter. Those of you who have read "The Rime of the Ancient Mariner" will remember that it tells of the disasters which came, one after another, to the vessel after the mariner had destroyed an albatross; how the crew finally hung the skeleton of the bird around his neck as a penalty. What a penalty that must have been, for aside from the condition of the bird, its weight and size were enough to kill the mariner. I have measured one which was 11 feet from the tip of one wing to the tip of the other, and which weighed 26 pounds.

The first albatross I remember seeing was swimming in the waters of the Southern Atlantic. We were on the *Erin's Isle*, making a trip from Rio de Janeiro to Australia and were about a week out from the former port when we came upon a number of them. I was very anxious to catch one and I did so with a simple hook and line and a piece of salt meat. I took the barb from the hook so that it would not penetrate the cheek of the bird and cause it pain. There was great excitement on board when I brought it in and the other members of the crew were very upset in case anything would happen to it. You see, they were remembering the ancient superstition and looked at me quite angrily as I announced my intention of retaining the albatross on board until I could learn more about it.

Although the food of this bird is squid, it ate salt meat and seemed to enjoy it. This I placed in a tub of clean salt water, for the creature will not eat anything which is not in water.

54

Yet, strangely enough, it seems to drink nothing, nor require it, for although it goes to shore or islands to nest, it is sometimes at sea for as long as eight or nine months without a drop of fresh water. Each time after eating, it washed out its beak, which amused me very much. The first few days it was seasick from the motion of the ship and would take nothing, but after that it seemed quite willing to trust me, and ate what I offered.

It was not necessary to keep the albatross in a pen or cage because it cannot take off in flight without a long run of perhaps 50 or 60 feet in calm weather. It is really like a living aeroplane and its ability to fly is affected strongly by the conditions of the weather.

The baby albatross is a beautiful thing to see. It is like a huge powder puff of seal brown. Neither head nor feet are visible. The down which covers it is about 2 inches long. With each moult it becomes more and more white and when old it is snow white with a flush of rose on the feathers of the neck. This rosy hue dies instantly at the death of the bird.

I can imagine that some member of my crew must have lain awake at night wondering with shivering and shaking what terrible fate would befall us if our captive died on board. Perhaps in his youth he had read "The Rime of the Ancient Mariner" and was troubled by the memory of it. Anyway, one morning when I went up on deck to look for my pet, it was gone. It couldn't leave the ship without being thrust overboard, and I felt very much like questioning my crew. But the bird was gone and it seemed unwise to make a fuss about it, so I noted what observations I had made and determined to make more the next time we came through that region. Perhaps I might have better luck again.

I had three golden plovers come on board one day when we were farther from shore than we had been when visited by any land bird before – over a thousand miles out, almost in mid-Pacific. Two of the plovers were utterly exhausted and died shortly after and when we examined their little stomachs, they were completely empty. The poor things had not fed for many days. It is wonderful that these small birds, and many other kinds of bird, make such long yearly flights without any compass to guide them, but the instinct which their Creator has given them. They are able to fly thousands of miles and to locate their landing without any of the instruments which sailors use, the same landing which they have made before, recognized from numberless others quite similar in appearance.

Hawks sometimes came on board and stayed with the ship for days if it were not too far from land. Their purpose was often to secure a meal from the body of some small bird blown out by winds and taking shelter with us. It was a pathetic sight to see the tiny songster, so happy at finding rest for his weariness, suddenly catch sight of his arch enemy, the hawk, and terrified of his life, start away in a vain effort to escape. The hawk was after him in a second, forcing him lower and lower until he touched the water, when with outspread legs and claws it would pounce on him, lifting him in its talons to a perch high up on the mast or rigging, there to be eaten in a minute of time. But there were times when the ocean, itself, seemed to resent the cruelty of the big bird and just as it secured its prey, a wave would wet its plumage so that it floundered helplessly and soon became the victim of some waiting sea creature as hungry as itself.

I tried to catch a hawk one night. He had perched on the Royal yard just at dusk and I waited until it was very dark and then went up armed with a bag to put over his head. I went up and up until I actually saw his form against the sky line, then crept cautiously up a few ratlines and farther on to the Royal foot-rope. I was very near him and had him in my hands, but I made a mistake which nearly cost me my life. I had thought of his beak but had forgotten his claws. And did he use them! Why I didn't let go, I don't know. It just didn't occur to me to do so. I gave his neck a tight squeeze through the bag and started to scramble down with him while his wind was cut off by the pressure. When I reached the deck one of the boys helped me to pry his strong claws loose and I tossed him into the boatswain's locker.

My wrist was bleeding terribly and it took some time to get it stopped and the wounds attended to. He had made a job of it and it was a fortunate thing for me that he had missed certain of the veins which might have caused more serious bleeding had they been cut. After that, when I tackled the hawk, which I did several times to make a study of the bird, I wore heavy gloves and wrapped my wrists well. After a week of observation I let him go without regret.

When we were in the port of Adelaide, in Australia, some of us on the ship bought birds as pets. There were many really magnificent birds to be had quite cheaply, among them a few of the parrot family which could be taught to talk, and a sulphur-crested cockatoo. I had been told that the cockatoo could be taught to talk better than even a parrot and I bought this beauty which was only a few months old.

I had an old round parrot cage on board, for one of the officers had taken a bird on another voyage, so the trader from whom I bought my bird put the cockatoo into that for me. He was very young, but I did not like the look of his beak nor his baleful eye. Unfortunately the cage was too small for him and he couldn't turn around without almost breaking the feathers of his tail. I decided to buy him a new cage the next time I was on shore.

When I found a cage that I considered suitable for my bird, the storekeeper wanted such a price for it that I made up my mind to make one as soon as I got to sea. We had plenty of old stayback wire and I was rather handy with a hammer. I was sorry to keep the bird in his cramped quarters even for a few days but it was really necessary.

I called him Togo, because he had the battle look in his eye and I imagined it was similar to the famous expression of the great Japanese Admiral of that day.

I thought by removing the perch I would give my bird a

57

little more room but when I took it out Togo hung by his feet from the top of the cage and screamed. He refused to stand on the floor and I had to replace the perch.

I was so busy that, try as I would, I couldn't get at the making of the new cage at once. At last, I drew up a plan and gave it to the ship's carpenter while I proceeded in my spare time to cut off and unstrand the four inch rigging wire. It took me two days to straighten this with a hammer. By that time the frame was finished. The carpenter gave me the pieces and I built it up.

It looked fine in frame, like a tiny hot-house. I showed it to Togo and asked him what he thought of it. For an answer he grabbed the food dish from me which I was about to hand to him and threw it onto the floor with a couple of war whoops that were loud enough to wake anyone in the Watch below. I said, "Look here, old man, if you do that too often, somebody will throw you overboard to the sharks."

When the wire "palace" was fully ready, the door of the old cage was brought into line with that of the new and a few prods of a ruler pushed Togo into his new domicile. Immediately when the door was closed he emitted a couple of his favourite yells with a "shiver my timbers" expression. I interpreted these as "thank you" and left him to himself for a while.

When I came down to the cabin in the evening, an afternoon storm was causing the ship to do considerable rolling. This sent the cage sliding about in a way which would never do. I at once jammed it off on a sort of broad shelf that extended across the stern of the ship against the lee wall. Next morning I would make a proper level with the back of the couch that formed the front of the transom, as a fastening for it. The floor of the transom was polished mahogany and the continuation of the cabin walls above it were panelled with the same wood and birds-eye maple, as were most of the ships of that day.

I went down after breakfast the next morning to fix up a proper place for the new cage and found that there were splinters and bits of wood all over the floor of the cage. These pieces were not from the wood of the frame, but mahogany, like the panels of the cabin wall. Then I saw what my "pet" had done. He had torn the whole edge off the mahogany mouldings as far as he could reach which was the full length of the cage. He had begun on the panels as well and had almost completely destroyed some of them, the wood of which could not be matched at any price.

I was very angry but had to blame myself for the way I had placed his cage. I took it down at once, putting it where he couldn't reach anything destructible, however far he might stretch his neck through the bars. He was not daunted by this, but began to tear up the floor of his home and to utter shrieks while doing so. He quieted down after a while and I thought he was through protesting.

A few days later, on a fine-weather day, I decided to bring him up on deck and the Mate came to help me. The cage was not heavy and Togo made no objection to being moved, but when we reached the cabin door we found the cage couldn't be got through. The carpenter had misread my measurements by 4 inches and those 4 inches were enough to spoil the whole thing.

I sat down on the top of the cage and felt pretty sick. The Mate was rather sarcastic. "What a pity," he said, "the poor innocent bird won't get his ultra violet rays and most likely he'll develop rickets."

"You may joke if you like," I told him, "but it's a nuisance all the same."

Just then my cockatoo make a peck at my leg which brought me to my feet. The Mate laughed. But the bird seemed to resent his applause and to take sides with me from that time on.

We were never able to get the cage onto deck but Togo lived on and became more contented. I began to really like him. He was definitely a beautiful creature and when he ruffled his crest he looked like an admiral wearing a plumed hat.

One afternoon as I walked the weather alleyway on deck,

I heard a frightful shriek from the cabin. I ran toward it. I knew the voice was Togo's, but I had never heard him shriek like that before. I made a sudden rush down the companionway but coming from the light into comparative darkness I could see nothing for a moment. Then I beheld a sight indeed. Togo was out of his cage, facing his image in the mirror, flapping his wings and yelling like fury. I made a dash toward him and he turned to fly past me. In those narrow quarters he seemed as big as a couple of eagles and as I dodged he gave me a bang on the nose with his wing. The steward, hearing the noise, dashed in to see what had happened, holding the door open. The bird saw the opening and made a swift dive in that direction. The steward fled before him fearing he might be hit in the face. He and the bird were up the companionway and on deck before me. I followed in time to see my cockatoo flying away to leeward over the ocean. As I watched him, he wheeled about and started back. I held my breath. He was returning to the ship! Would he reach it? His wings were very weak for he had not been exercising them. At less than 6 feet from the vessel, caught by the down draught of the sails, he fell into the sea.

# The Mighty Whale

Wonderful things have been done in little ships. Take for example the ships which whalers used in my early days. They were built in the Maritimes and in the New England States, especially on New Brunswick shores and on those of Massachusetts.

These ships were not only little in comparison with the sailing ships to which I was accustomed, but they were ship-rigged. The small vessels of the '80's and '90's were either brigs or brigantines, but the whaling men would have nothing like that. They wanted full-rigged ships and they got them.

I remember one ship which I saw in Talcahuano. She was called the *Fane Stewart* and had the appearance of a big model, not a real ship at all. She looked something like an express wagon would look beside a good-sized family car.

It always seems funny to me that men should use such small boats to catch or hunt whales, the biggest animal in the ocean, and when they reached whaling waters, they got into even tinier boats, row boats, to search for the big game. The whale was big, make no mistake about that.

We read a lot about the giant creatures that walked the land and inhabited the sea during the long bygone geological period. One gazes in awe at their fossils or their reconstructed life-sized models in museums. But the greatest creature in size that has ever appeared on this globe is one of the whale family and still to be found – the sperm whale. The skeleton of this species is not found in museums. Perhaps that is why its immensity is often forgotten when considering the history of prehistoric animals.

The earlier explorers and voyagers said so much about the size of the sperm whale that we got to the point of not believing them. There was for instance the tale of someone who mistook one of these creatures for an island and proceeded to land there and to build himself a fire, only to discover that this island was in motion and sinking slowly under him into the sea. Another story even more unbelievable was that of a sailor who sailed his ship right into a gaping cavern at midday only to find himself in a pit of darkness. He had entered the whale's open mouth. Except for such exaggerations little has been told about the sperm whale, but we do find references to it in Melville's *Moby Dick*.

When I was skipper of the *Arctic Stream*, I saw two of these sperm whales. They were swimming along peacefully side by side only 100 feet or so from our ship. They were parallel with her and travelling at the same rate of speed. It was a wonderful sight.

Their colour is called white but it is really a light grey. White whales have been seen in the Arctic and in the St. Lawrence Gulf but they do not belong to the same species. They were probably relatives of the one described in *Moby Dick*.

From the deck of the *Arctic Stream* the two whales looked as long as the ship herself and as they edged nearer and nearer to her, my heart was in my mouth. I hoped that they were not bad tempered and that they did not remember the ill treatment given to their ancestors. They finally rubbed against the ship. I was glad when Old Peter, one of the sailors who had often been on whaling ships, came to look over the rail with me. He said they were rubbing against us to rid themselves of barnacles, but added, "I don't mind so long as they don't take it into their heads to rub against the rudder and break it off."

This could have easily happened if the ship had lifted out of the sea pushing the rudder against them.

After Old Peter spoke, I thought of many things that could happen if a creature some 130-odd feet long and weighing possibly 150 tons should lose its temper. I felt the ship quiver and then our visitors moved off and disappeared into the vastness of the ocean wastes.

We were fortunate indeed. Our ship, though steel and some 240 feet long, might easily have been damaged had the whales charged at a charging speed of 25 miles an hour. We might have sprung a leak serious enough to sink us.

Some years later, near the Equator, I had another adventure with a whale. This was a full-grown ordinary female sperm whale and it had its baby with it. The baby was about 30 feet long and 7 or 8 feet thick.

I had often shot at whales when on the surface, but they had not paid any attention. Although in the case of a very large one, I had succeeded in hitting it several times. I used a big game rifle. The whale lay very still. "Ah," thought I, "I must have wounded you in a vital spot this time." To make sure, I fired two more shots into the whale (as I thought). The creature moved lazily, sort of yawned as if I had interrupted its afternoon nap and swam away.

The day I sighted the mother and baby, there was very little wind and the ship was moving slowly. I thought if the small one came near enough I might be able to kill it and so get a few barrels of valuable oil. They were swimming some distance apart, far enough for the ship to pass between them. When the little one came up to blow or breathe, I fired three bullets into it.

It stopped. Believing I had killed it I got ready to put out in one of our boats with the idea of capturing it before it sank. Suddenly it gave a couple of wild leaps and turned around looking for its mother, just as a hurt child might have done. Now what was going to happen?

It came up against the side of the boat and gave it a few

nasty wallops with its tail. I could not take any chances. I quickly fired the remaining shells in the magazine into its back. The young animal seemed to realize that it must disappear below the surface if it would escape further hurt and it sank down rapidly below the vessel. From there, no doubt, it spied its mother and made for her as fast as it could to be comforted. I was sorry that I had caused pain, perhaps serious injury to no purpose.

Soon the freshening breezes carried us miles from the locality and even if the parent had wanted to punish us she would have had a hard time catching up with us.

The whale, often wrongly referred to as a fish, is a warm-blooded mammal like the elephant. It has to come to the surface to breathe. Fish do not require to do this, but the whale has a very complicated breathing apparatus made to do all sorts of unexpected things. The apparatus is designed so that the great pressure of the water when the whale is deep down in the ocean does not cause it any inconvenience. The apparatus is a study in itself.

When the whale comes to the surface to blow, it plainly shows the hunter where it is.

This blowing is just the letting out of heated and compressed air from its lungs. This air is visible only as vapour and not as a column of actual water as many used to believe and as some pictures show it. True, there is sometimes a little water in it because the whale often releases it just before its nose appears above the surface. The blowing of a whale is usually accompanied by quite a loud noise, a sort of "whish" that in calm weather may be heard over a distance of several miles.

To have a whale blow unexpectedly close by a ship on a calm night is a terrifying sound, resembling the sigh of a vast giant several times the size of a man. If the whale is to windward, the musky odour of its breath is very noticeable after the blow.

When we see a number of birds flying together we speak of them as a flock, a number of wolves or dogs are referred to as a pack. When we speak of a number of whales we call them a pod. It seems natural to refer to a pod of peas or beans, but a pod of whales . . . that term always struck me as a funny one.

Speaking of whales in general, they are a pretty gentle, good-humoured lot of giants and do not injure or destroy for the love of doing so. They are carnivorous it is true, that is, they live on the flesh of other animals, but these they kill for food and not for the sport of killing.

However, these whales have an outlaw relative—the black sheep of the family. This species hunts and kills for the sheer love of destroying life. It is fittingly called the killer whale and is the largest distinctly wicked creature in the ocean. It is much smaller than the true whales, rarely over 25 feet in length, more slim than any of its relatives, and very swift in motion. Its teeth resemble those of an enormous wolf and it acts much like a wolf in that it hunts in packs, and strange to say, it likes most to hunt its big relation, the true whale.

The true whale keeps its mouth open most of the time. It does this so that the water will pour into the mouth and out again through the sides of the jaws where the whale-bone strainer catches all small living things. These creatures make for the whale a kind of living stew. Its throat is very small and only tiny fish and microscopic life can slip down. The hanging lower jaw acts as a sort of scoop while the true whale swims through the shoals of small fish. The mouth is closed while this straining operation goes on.

The killer whale knows this habit of its relative and attacks unexpectedly when the mouth is open, seizing the lower lips with great teeth and holding on like a bull-dog. Another of its number rushes into the open mouth and bites out the tongue, which is their special fancy. As if this were not enough they then bite great chunks out of its body.

Another favourite food of the killer whale is seal meat. The seal is a fast swimmer itself and can catch nearly any fish in the water but when a couple of killer whales spot it, it hasn't a chance unless it is able to reach an ice-floe, beach, or rock, and hurl itself on it. If the seals take refuge on a floe of ice, the killer whales are not discouraged. They combine forces and rush up under the ice, breaking it through. If the ice is in a huge cake, one of them will tip up the cake while another waits for the seal to slip off into the water.

In Shackleton's book on the Antarctic there is a vivid description of such a hunt. In this case the creature hunted was not a seal but a man whom the killers had mistaken for a seal. He escaped by a very narrow margin indeed when one of the ship's cutters came to his rescue armed with machine gun and harpoons. This story continues, that whales sometimes mistake the white-painted ship's boat for a cake of ice and the dark-coloured objects in it for seals. In this case they will readily attack if the boat does not move swiftly away.

I had a very narrow escape myself but did not realize how narrow until years after when I read Mr. Shackleton's story.

One day when I was in command, my ship was sailing slowly and silently over a glass-like South Pacific, waltzed along by a zephyr Trade Wind. I saw something ahead of us disturbing the surface. There were a few huge splashes and I then caught sight of dark bodies swiftly passing and re-passing one another in the water.

There is no mistaking the killer whale. He is peculiarly marked; an almost black body with white below and a distinct white band as a collar.

As the ship neared, I saw that there were several whales and that the water in which they were moving was stained with great patches of red blood. I was in an adventurous mood and curious to know what they were about. I ordered the boat lowered, which, like Shackleton's, was painted white. With four apprentices I jumped in and we pulled away ahead of our slowly moving ship to investigate.

The whales were dashing about this way and that, tearing and devouring huge hunks of red flesh, hunks some three feet square, and almost as thick, weighing a couple of hundred pounds apiece. It was clear that they had just killed a whale for the pieces were too large to have been bitten from anything else. In a few minutes the last morsel was gone. But the killers remained in motion, rushing about as if looking for something more. Then they saw us. One shot past our boat within a few feet and it gave us quite a start; then another. There was something about the look of them, about the cold expressionless eyes fixed upon us, which was not pleasant to see. As one grazed the boat I noted a row of wicked looking teeth showing as if in a grin. I shouted to the boys. "This is enough for me; we'll go back." But our ship had come up slowly on us and the killers sheered off from the larger moving body. We were so hypnotized by the creatures that we had not observed the vessel and it was almost on top of us before we noticed it. In another second the massive steel cut-water would have rolled us over into the mouths of these "gentle wolves."

Quickly the boys seized the oars and turned the boat parallel with the approaching ship and let her glide slowly by until we could seize the tackles hanging from the davits. The crew mustered by the officer in charge, soon hoisted the boat, and frapped her in. We climbed out of her with sighs of relief.

Not long after that I read of the killer's method of hunting seals and the cold shivers travelled up and down my spine. I realized that if it had not been for the timely arrival of the ship, we should soon have disappeared.

# How Sailing Ships Were Built

My father often talked to me about the things he remembered of the shipyards of his grandfather. Some famous ships were constructed in that part of the Maritimes, among them the *Marco Polo*. After school and on holidays, my father was seldom away from the shipyards where he watched his own father building a craft on which he himself was later to begin his seafaring career.

In the early days, a shipbuilder had to know how to construct every part of a ship. Today, he is generally limited to the knowledge of how to perfect only one part. When the ship was launched and finished, the builder often sailed his ship himself. It was his pride.

It was great amusement to watch the ship grow. Its beginning was not in the yards but in the forest. The first and most important job was done by the master-builder or woodsman, who with his assistants, went through the nearby forests, as a timber surveyor might do today, to select special trees for special purposes.

Not all one kind of timber can be used in the building of a ship. The straight or near-straight parts were selected from trees marked for that purpose by the master-builder and his men. These were spruce and pitch-pine for spars, beams, yards, and planking, oak for ribs or frames, and sometimes birch for planking the upper part. Then a special man made rounds to find trees with roots and branches bent sharply in a certain way which could not be done by steaming. These were used to make knees, transoms, and breast-hooks, and were severed from the trees by hand with great crosscut saws.

The marked trees were cut down, hauled out, and stacked in the shipyards. The hauling was mostly done in the winter over snow roads. Shipyards were usually on sloping ground near the river or bay into which the ship would be later launched. Here the timber was cut and prepared.

If it were the first ship to be built in that place, keel blocks had to be laid. These were squared timbers, 12 to 14 inches square and 4 or 5 feet long, laid one on top of the other to a height of about 4 feet, and spaced anywhere from 3 to 6 feet apart, with a good solid foundation under each one. These extended in a row right to the water's edge, sometimes a short distance into the water. The foundation under the blocks had to be a solid one because the keel was laid on top of them, and by the time the ship was built, they were under a tremendous weight. If they sank into the ground, or altered their position, this would cause a strain on the ship under construction. This was liable to damage her and would mean a great loss of money, as well as of time in repairing.

The laying of the timbers for the keel, especially if the vessel were the first to be built by a certain family or the first in that locality, was an event of great importance to the whole community. Schools were closed and the day was proclaimed a holiday. Many of the people were deeply religious folk and very often a simple religious ceremony was held over the keel-laying. In those days, there were more "family" ships than "company" ships and often the men who assisted in building and rigging, sailed as captain and crew. It is easily seen, then, why each workman took a personal interest and pride in making the structure strong and seaworthy, for was it not to carry his friends and himself over the oceans in all weathers? From its cargoes, he hoped to make a living for those he loved, and to bring prosperity to the community.

As building progressed, the ends and frames or ribs, which had been hewn to the required shapes, were erected. This was hard to accomplish.

When safely launched, the ship was taken by steam tugs, or hauled if none were available, to a wharf or berth where she was completed if not complete. Perhaps at the same berth she would be loaded with lumber in the form of deals of 3-inch planks, generally for Liverpool, England. The reason for going there was not only to take a cargo but to secure a more important cargo—salt.

Liverpool was a great salt exporting port and a cargo of this commodity was very useful because it salted the ship as the ship sailed. It was taken, usually, back to Canada for the purpose of salting other wooden ships. For actual salting, it was put between the frames of the ship in such a way that it would not slip right to the bottom, but stayed there and dissolved slowly in the moist air over a period of several years. The salt preserved the wood from rotting. This was done to the good old *Landseer* before we left Liverpool for India.

These may not be exciting facts but I wanted you to understand something of the construction of vessels which have never been equalled in beauty or in speed under sail.

I am proud that the famous *Marco Polo*, a marvellous Canadian ship, was built by James Smith, in Courtney Bay, New Brunswick. She was built the year the Dixon family became interested in shipbuilding—1851. At that time, my grandfather was getting out the timbers for his ships, the *Forest Queen*, a moderate-sized, full-rigged ship that was launched in 1853, and the big ship, the *Sarah Dixon*, which I told you about before, launched in 1856.

The *Marco Polo* was bought by James Bains of Liverpool, England, and was the pioneer ship of his famous fleet. It was sailed to Australia under the command of the skipper, Bully Forbes.

One day a dock-pilot met Mr. Bains on the street in Liverpool.

"I hear that the *Marco Polo* is just off the bar light, coming in," he said.

Mr. Bains laughed incredulously–"Think of you hearing a thing like that. Why man, I haven't heard of her arrival in Australia yet." But he hurried down to the pier head, just the same, and the man was right! It was the *Marco Polo* bringing in the mail which contained the news of her own arrival in Australia, after making the fastest voyage by a sailing ship ever known. She established the supremacy of Bains' Ball Line and Canadian built ships. Even the famous *Lightning*, said to be the fastest vessel ever built to be driven by the wind, in actual speed for days' runs, did not lower the *Marco Polo*'s record to and from Australia.

Although the *Lightning* was built in the United States she was constructed by men who were Canadian by birth. They had not received the recognition they sought here and they went across the border. The *Lightning* made her famous run on March 11th, 1854, crossing the Atlantic, a distance of 436 nautical miles, 502 land miles, at the rate of 18 knots or 20.9 land miles per hour. Captain Forbes of the *Marco Polo* was the man in charge of her at this time. When they hove the log, the line was often too short for the terrific speed and when it came to the end of the reel, the jerk was so fierce that it was quite an easy matter for the one holding the reel to be jerked overboard before he could let go. So when Captain Forbes called out, "What's she makin', Mister?" the Mate would shout back, "Eighteen and the Boy, sir." At that high rate of speed, it was vital to turn the log-glass at the exact fraction of second when "Turn" was shouted.

Sometimes when it was desired to report untruly a faster speed than the ship was making, it was rumoured some such trick as the following was played: the Mate would shout, "Turn" as the stray-line mark passed the rail. The man holding the log-glass would call back, "Did you say to turn, sir?" The Mate would reply, "Yes, you dumb cluck," or words more forcible, and the man would answer, "Turn it is, sir." By this time, at least 3 extra knots had gone by. Then when the sand had run out, the man would shout, "Stop," and the Mate would say, "Did you say stop?" "Yes, sir," from the man. Then the Mate would respond, "Stop it is." By that time another three additional knots had run out at this end as well. So, if the ship were going 12 knots, the Mate reported 18 knots in the logbook. There wasn't much satisfaction in such deception, at least to honest fellows. It was said, also, that some wonderful speeds were reported by towing two logs and adding the readings together, the same as if you had two speedometers on your car and each registered 40 and you said you were doing 80.

But although there may have been some dishonesty, it still remains true that the clipper ships were the most beautiful and the fastest ships that ever sailed the seas.

A few years later the Patent-log came into use, with a rotator and dial like a gas-meter.

In very early days, the Phoenicians used a special kind of log which British and American sailors sometimes substituted for the kind more commonly used, if the ship was nearly becalmed and going too slowly for the hand-log or the Patent-log. I have often used this kind, myself, and found it reliable, but my use of it was somewhat different to theirs. Their way was to go near the bow of the ship, throw a chip of wood overboard or something that would float, and walk along the deck as the ship went ahead, keeping pace with the floating object. They judged the rate of speed by the rate at which they walked. My way was to have a man at a certain spot for'ard, drop the chip overboard at a measured distance from the spot where I stood and to time by watch how long it took the ship to go that distance. On my ship, I had the measured distance 152 feet or one-fortieth of a nautical mile. I think it is the same method as that used by sailors in Bible times, but having no watches, they just walked along with the floating chip.

In my old packets, we made some mighty good runs, almost equal to that of the fliers about which we have been talking.

One packet, the *Arctic Stream* sailed 3,913 nautical miles (or 4,506 statute miles) in 15 days, an average of 260 nautical miles or 329.2 statute miles per day. On another voyage from Rio de Janeiro to Australia for eleven days she averaged 267 nautical miles or 307 statute miles per day, breaking the record made on a previous sail of one day and 9 hours. I record this proudly.

# I Become a Crew Member

The *Erin's Isle*, on which I shipped as a deck boy, had been built by a famous shipbuilder, John McFee. His wife and son William sailed regularly with him. William, in manhood, became the author of many excellent books about the sea and seafaring.

As Boy, I was a proud though humble member of the *Erin's Isle* crew. It was I who struck the bell on the poop. It was I who kept the binnacle lit and supplied with oil. The binnacle lights were important to the man at the wheel. They helped him to read the ship's compass.

But an experienced helmsman steered as much by the wind as by the compass. He kept an eye upon the wind's effect on the after sails. In a storm or during a heavy sea, it some-times took two or even three men to control the wheel in or-der to hold the ship to her course.

Each sailor was supposed to take a 2-hour turn at the wheel daily. If inexperienced, the Mate or one of the senior crew stood by.

A few times I asked for the privilege of steering and I still feel a surge of pride when I recall my first successful attempt. There was a following sea and it was heavy going, but when the Mate put his hand on the wheel to help me, I said, "Please let me do it. I can do it alone. I know I can."

But when a few minutes later the ship began to heel, I gave over willingly.

"You'll do fine in time, Boy," the Mate said kindly.

Many challenges were before me. I had to meet them with outward courage at least. I had never been aloft. The first such experience came on our sail from Rio de Janeiro to Calcutta.

We were crossing the Indian Ocean and there we suffered from several gales. One afternoon the Mate told me to overhaul the gear on the royal. I started to climb and as I neared the top mast I found myself looking down with some apprehension. It seemed to me that I was not over the ship at all but over the sea. I experienced a feeling of terror.

The Mate was watching me. "Don't look down, Boy," he shouted. I obeyed him. Setting my teeth I performed the work which he had sent me to do. As I finished, such a sense of achievement and relief came over me that I would have one look, now, before climbing down. One look was enough for the waves were enormous and I saw that we were in for another gale. Although climbing down was difficult, I performed this business as quickly as I could. I drew a sigh of thankfulness when I felt the deck beneath my feet, but I met the Mate's eyes proudly. I had been aloft!

When I recall the many storms encountered by the *Erin's Isle*, I marvel that she survived them. Each voyage supplied another test of strength. There was, for example, her second sail into equatorial waters.

We left New York the beginning of April and when nearly over to the Western Islands, we sailed south. It had been rough weather most of the way and we had seen little sea life except a variety of gulls.

Although still only a deck boy, I was developing a growing interest in the behaviour of creatures in, on, and over the sea. I had always been fascinated by my father's "Log and Remark" book and I began to keep a sort of diary of my own observations.

It was during a fierce gale just before we crossed the Equator that for the first time I caught sight of the stormy petrel, about which I have written elsewhere. It was so named, I am sure, because it seemed to belong to the storm.

Storms harassed us during a large part of the voyage. Therefore, I had little time for observations of beast or bird. We were in for another blow and although I was really off watch, the Mate ordered me to remain with him. Already the top gallant was being clewed up and furled. The sea was beginning to make with a proper winter storm. Soon our ship was throwing spray high and the tops of tall waves came on board as she plunged along southward. Before darkness fell real seas were boarding us with such force that we were frequently swept from our feet. Drenched and half-frozen, the men struggled with the gear of the mainsail before going aloft to furl it. In our wet state the bitter cold wind chilled us to the marrow, but no one thought of his discomfort until all had been done for our good ship that could be done.

It was on the *Erin's Isle* during such weather that I shared in duties which prepared me to later become an experienced A.B.

When the gale abated and we were relieved for a time at least, I came in for my portion of the hot cocoa waiting for us in the galley. A few grumbled that they would have preferred a "tot of rum" but for some reason my father, as "skipper," kept to his opinion that cocoa properly made and steaming hot was the revival drink for his crew.

The spell of bad weather lasted for almost a full week, then it passed and we were away before the steady wind of the northeast Trades.

In the South Pacific en route to Cape Horn, bound for the Equatorial Regions, we were approaching the lands where cocoa can be grown. The tree is small and temperamental, like a fussy invalid. It must have a climate of around 80 degrees, never below 60 nor over 100, with a nice amount of rainfall for the year, and spread out in a particular way. Other kinds of trees are planted to shade it from too hot sun and to shelter it from strong winds.

The fruit of the "cacao" tree contains the seeds from which cocoa is made. Linnaeus, the famous Swedish naturalist and botanist who established our scientific system of naming plants and animals, called cocoa "a food for the gods."

That which was used on ships of my day was not the delicately flavoured product which appears in grocery stores today. Navy or rock cocoa, a favourite drink in sailing ships, had most of the oil pressed from it and was fashioned into hard cakes. When powdered and mixed with water and milk and sweetened with sugar it was rich, nourishing, and delicious to the taste, but very strong for even sailors' stomachs to tolerate until they became accustomed to it. This cocoa had a heating quality which I do not find in the modern product. It seemed to spread into every part of the body and to refresh it.

Our Second Mate, McWilliams, was especially fond of cocoa and because he liked to make himself a private drink of it, he kept several cakes in his locker. The cakes were wrapped in brown paper and tied with string.

The *Erin's Isle* had two Boys, Tom Manley and myself. We were usually around somewhere when the smell of cocoa was in the air, and Mr. McWilliams knew that we were aware of his hiding place for the precious stuff.

One evening after a trip to his locker he met us with angry looks and language which he seldom used. He had found his locker in a mess with torn paper and pieces of string mixed with bits of chewed cloth and scraps of wood. It was dark and with only a match to see by, all he seemed to realize was the absence of his cocoa cakes. He had a small oil stove in his room and Tom and I had smelt the burning oil. We were not far from his door, hoping that he would share with us. Suspiciously, he turned on us, believing we had stolen from him. He grabbed Tom first and dealt him a rope's ending. I would be next. I slipped behind them and fished in his locker.

In the handful of rubbish which I gathered quickly I felt something hard. It was a piece of cocoa cake, alright, and when I held it to the light a neat row of tooth marks on the piece was all the evidence needed. But the riddled condition of the wrappings provided more.

As the rope ending struck Manley a third time, I yelled, "Mr. McW—look here." I held the rat-marked cocoa cake out to him.

"Rats," I said. "Not us—rats."

He took the piece of cake and held it to the light. "I'm blowed if I don't believe you're right," he said. He apologized to Manley. In his room, we carved off the outside of the cake. In his locker we found more damaged pieces and did the same with them.

Soon Mr. McWilliams, Tom Manley and myself were drinking cocoa together.

He filled an extra mug and handed it to me. "Take this up to the Mate," he said. "It's a devil of a night, but don't mention the rats."

The Mate was standing under the weather cloth in the mizzen rigging while spray and sheets of rain eddied around him.

"Thanks, Boy," he said.

"Mr. McWilliams sent it, sir," I told him.

"But you brought it and you're off watch," he observed.

We had some fine men in our crew.

The cacao or cocoa tree does not bear fruit until it is seven years old, and then maybe only one pound of beans. Much patience and many manoeuvres go into the making of one cup of cocoa—planting, long careful cultivating and harvesting, followed by the difficult business of transporting, and then the manufacturing.

Humans are not the only ones who like cocoa. While the fruit is maturing it has to be guarded from such raiders as parrots, armadillos and monkeys.

From where it was grown to a port of sailing it was often carried in bags on the shoulders or heads of natives marching for many miles through jungles and rough country inhabited by dangerous insects and wild animals. Sometimes it was packed in barrels and rolled for miles and miles through forest paths to the nearest port; then there was the long journey by sea often in the damp, musty hold of some old wooden ship.

Fed well from the galley and warmed thoroughly by hot cocoa when the stormy cold winds and heavy rains made life miserable, we were a fairly contented crew. There was occasional grumbling but if deep discontents existed they were well hidden.

# The Magic Tree

I want to tell you about an island in the South Pacific, thousands of miles from a mainland, though having a few fairy-like isles within a hundred miles or so. This was the first time that I found myself among the wonderful trees common to that part of the world. They grow in many other places but do not seem to have such magic properties.

I shall skip ahead a bit in time but that is of no significance when one is voyaging to a Pacific isle. I went there aboard the *Arctic Stream* as its skipper.

We were sailing down the Pacific to Portland, Oregon, and thence to England. We were in the area of the Trade Winds. It was a truly tropical morn. Away to the western horizon there was a very narrow strip of greenish sky parallel with and just above the line of visibility. The Trade Winds were very light.

Almost as we watched, the clear line between ocean and sky became roughened and in a few minutes the roughness became individual lumps like half tiny beads and the green strip grew wider and much longer. The use of our binoculars showed these lumps to be tops of palms and the green the reflection from the emerald waters of a coral lagoon.

In about an hour's time we were near enough to see the groves of palms, the snow-like beach, the band of white surf beating on the windward side of the island, and the shading blues from light to dark from the island seaward, until the ultra-marine of ocean depths was reached. The sight was one which none of us would ever forget.

To our crew who had seen nothing but sea and sky for weeks, this was the nearest thing to an earthly paradise that we could imagine.

As we sailed around the leeward side, the trade winds dropped to an almost calm. What we were approaching, according to sailing directions, was supposed to be inhabited but up to now we had seen no one.

In very short order the gig was launched and four apprentices, the carpenter and myself, slid down the tackles into the boat. We cast off and pulled for the nearest point of land. As we approached, we altered our course, making for what looked to be a fair landing place. When we drew near, it did not look so good. As the swell fell back from the reef and exposed the sharp ragged edge and overhanging face of the reef, it certainly did not look inviting. Pulling along parallel with the shore, we noted that this appeared very much the same. It might have discouraged us in attempting a landing but we were determined. We knew, however, that if we misjudged the time in going in, we would land on that coral edge and be smashed to pieces for the patrolling sharks to pick up.

I did not give my imagination time to brood on the dangers, but swinging the boat ahead around towards the reef, on the next incoming swell, I gave the order to "give way." The boys bent to their oars and in a few seconds the boat was flying like an arrow on the crest of the swell which got steeper as it approached the reef. As the swell broke the boat went even faster over the reef which was now under shallow water.

I shouted to the bow men, "In oars and jump when I give the word."

In a couple of seconds the ingoing water stopped and I shouted again, "Jump."

The two boys and the carpenter who was in the bow with them, leaped into the shallow water on the reef and held the boat against the now outgoing stream until the water had sunk and we grounded on the coral.

The others in the boat together with myself took in the oars and, leaping into the now foot-deep water on the reef, followed the bowmen and the carpenter.

A second swell now rushed toward us, immersing us in water up to our waists. We stood by to guide the boat in farther. We did not have to lift her. She lifted us as she was carried landward. On the last of the ingoing stream we rushed her into the shallows until she grounded. Now she was safe.

We now saw to our amazement a man and three women, one carrying a small child, with two children trailing along behind. The children had picked up the painter, the rope by means of which a boat is towed or moored. The carpenter had taken the rope on ahead to tie to a tree, with the purpose of insuring that the boat would not be carried back by the rushing water. He signalled to the children that we did not want the boat to go any farther. Pulling by them would even have forced it farther up onto the sandy beach which began at the end of the coral.

"She's safe now, for sure," I said. "But I hope these people will help us to get her off again for we'll never manage it alone from here."

We crossed the beach. The whiteness of it nearly blinded us. It was more white and glistening than the whitest snow.

The man gave us a sign to follow him. He led us to where three palms stood together and the shade of the trees was a relief to our eyes.

When the man spoke, it was in what might be called island French, or "Bêche-de-mer" as the novelists like to call it. None of us knew more than a few words of ordinary French, but in a sort of sign language, and a manufactured Esperanto, we were quickly understood. He spoke to us then in simple sentences.

He was clothed in bleached blue overalls and the women in universal island style in coloured print slips or gowns. The clothing indicated some contact with island traders. In keeping with the climate and their surroundings, the children were wholly unclothed.

We noticed two huts not far away and now we were led toward them. As we approached we were met by a dog, two pigs, and a flock of hens. Such was our deputation of welcome.

Outside the huts and within was evidence of the importance to these people of the magic tree, the coconut palm. The huts were built of its leaves; leaves also formed the beds. Hanging from the walls and resting on the floor were various vessels, all of them made from the outside shell of the fruit. The meat of the nut provided food for man and beast. The immature fruit was similar in consistency to a soft blancmange, and the milk which could be drained from the nut by puncturing the shell formed the favourite beverage.

Utensils used for cleaning, such as brushes and scrapers, are made from the palm tree. Lamps are used for light. They are also made from the tree, even to the wick and the oil. Equipment for fishing is a product of the trunk of the tree—the nets and the lines.

Crab meat is consumed by the islanders, but since the crabs feed upon the coconut palm they, too, may be said to be a food from the tree. Of course fish and fowl provide additional food. But the mainstay of the island, a tree which the natives all but worship, is the prevalent coconut palm.

The dependence of the people upon the coconut can be better understood when we realize that from it they derived their only substitute for water which is not otherwise available to them. The only fresh water was that caught from dripping roofs of huts during a rainfall but unless it was carefully stored, it was soon unpalatable. What fell upon the coral sank through and mixed with the salt water of the ocean.

Occasional severe storms destroy many of the older trees. Only the younger ones can survive. But the natives were continually planting coconuts to raise more trees and they refused to trade a coconut tree although they were eager to secure articles brought by travellers and were generous enough with everything else.

Unaware of this feeling, I looked about me for a small tree to carry back to the ship with the intention of planting it in a tub and studying its growth. I attempted to pull up a tiny sapling but was stopped by a shout from a native. "No, no," he cried. I had to be satisfied with a couple of fully ripened nuts.

I pointed to a wedge shaped stick driven into the ground. There were many of these. One of the natives explained in sign language that these were used for splitting open the coconut husks. The eyes of the shell were punctured with another sharp stick or pointed knife.

This is indeed a marvellous tree and certainly is a tree of life, but it provides a mighty monotonous diet for there is practically no other growing thing which is used as food. For breakfast you have a couple of split coconuts, for lunch ditto, and when the children ask for a snack between meals they are given a section from the nut. The evening meal is a repetition of the others. We felt that one can get too much of anything.

Although we could not buy a coconut tree we managed to make a deal for several other things. I traded a shirt which I had brought from our small stock of goods known as the slop chest. This stock was kept on hand for the master of the ship to sell to the crew. For the shirt I secured two pigs and some chickens. I added a few plugs of tobacco for which I received hens and a few coconuts.

I asked if he had any pearls for sale, although I had not seen any diving apparatus about and this was therefore unlikely. Since diving for pearls can be done only by the young and strong and all but two of the adults were past middle age, I was prepared for a negative answer, but I received an agreeable surprise. He went into the hut and brought out a small shell wrapped in calico. He unwrapped it and there were several pearls of various sizes but not perfect specimens. For two pearls, I traded a few ordinary sailors' knives. But when I showed

84

him a small hatchet, which I always included in our equipment, in case we encountered a shark or other dangerous fish, he became very excited and gave me all the pearls he had left for it. One was a beauty.

In the meantime the boys and the carpenter were trading knives and their belts with the women for small curios and also a few pearls.

Our attention had been on trading but now we noted that the boat was drifting away from the island which meant that we must now launch the small boat and set off at once. It was quite a distance to row.

I signified to our new friends that we must leave and they all came down to help turn the small boat around and to get her near the edge of the reef. We couldn't stop to consider possible dangers but they were obvious to us all. We watched for the first outgoing swell. The instant the swell started to flow seaward, we hopped in the boat, shipped the oars, and were thankful for the push which the men gave us. We rowed frantically and in a few seconds were beyond the break of the next incoming swell. We were now safely on our way to our floating home, cheerily waving our goodbyes to the natives of a magic island.

We unloaded our cargo of livestock into the gig, but I should add that not all of it was still alive. Our boat had shipped quite a bit of water when making a dive off the reef and the chickens were submerged. The pigs were still above water but making a loud complaint, in pig language, telling us all about it.

The boys were pleased that the fowl were dead because now they would be sure of a chicken dinner. Had the chickens remained alive, one at a time would have been killed and served only to the captain's table.

Soon our gig was speeding toward the waiting ship. We reached it at twilight, hoisted the boat and went aboard. By the time it was completely dark we were on our way to the far distant Cape Horn with its cold, its storms and other discomforts.

Astern, as daylight faded, all that was visible of our magic island were the plumes of the noble coconut palms. Soon they too faded into the rapidly gathering gloom. I turned and went below with a distinct sense of loneliness and busied myself in planting the two ripest coconuts in a tub filled with island sand.

One of the coconuts sprouted and grew finely until the cold of the Cape Horn region chilled its vitals and it curled up and died.

# *We Visit Rio*

On my first voyage to Rio de Janeiro I was an ordinary seaman. The ship was the *Erin's Isle* and my father was her Captain. We took a cargo of barrelled oil from New York to Liverpool.

When we were leaving New York our ship had her top gallant sails up. It was necessary to take these down in order to pass under Brooklyn Bridge. While we were replacing them we sent up the Royal yard also. We had an inexperienced crew on this voyage so the Second Mate went up to supervise. His helper had joined up only the day before but he had a full year of sailing behind him. However, he didn't care for deck work and was to have become assistant to the cook the following day.

The two men were working 160 feet aloft. As they endeavoured to put the Royal yard across, the lift gave way. They were thrown to the deck. The younger man died instantly and the Second Mate was critically injured. Fortunately, we met an incoming steamer a few minutes later with a doctor on board. He came to our aid and at once the Second Mate was removed to the steamer and taken to a hospital in New York, but he did not recover.

Seamen know the perils of working aloft and we accepted tragedy as an inevitable part of life at sea but I think we all suffered from a feeling of apprehension during the balance of our run to Liverpool. We had a good ship and my father as skipper was a man of good judgement, but by accident and storm, many a fine ship and capable crew have been lost. Danger was a part of seafaring and yet it might be said that we loved the great oceans even while we feared them.

A few days after we had lost two members of our crew we ran into a storm which had been harassing ships that crossed the North Atlantic for more than a month. It tossed up waves of frightening power while torrents of rain came from lowering dark skies. That voyage was one of the most unpleasant and depressing which I experienced in 34 years of sailing. We sighted England's shores with relief.

Before leaving Liverpool for Rio we discharged our cargo of oil and took on one of bone meal; also my father hired two sailors from a disabled American ship in dock for long repairs, to replace the members of our crew whom we had lost by death.

We all thought it a good omen when we set sail from Liverpool under clear skies with a bright sun shining. The wind was kind and a pair of canaries given to my father by an English friend sang cheerily from a sparred cage firmly attached to a wooden shelf in his cabin.

It was not the first time he had taken birds to sea and later I was to follow his example.

We ran into good weather the better part of the way—a few storms, of course, but none to compare with those which we had suffered in more northern waters. However, as we approached Rio we met with a more serious threat to our survival.

Rio de Janeiro possessed a magnificent harbour. We moored the *Erin's Isle* in the part known as Gamboa. With two anchors down, our ship when swung by wind or tide, moved in a small circle which allowed other vessels to be moored quite near. We counted 48 ships in port from all parts of the world.

On an island quite near to us was a hospital for smallpox victims, a dreaded disease which was rampant at the time. Prevalent, too, was yellow fever. It was said that thousands died of these diseases that year. The dead had been buried in a great lime pit at the back of the hospital. Drainage from the city poured into the waters close by. When there was a land wind, the odours were horrible. Today Rio is one of the most beautiful and healthy tropical cities in the world.

There was a landing place near where we had located, and another close to the centre of the city.

Rio was subject to many thunder-storms and accompanying squalls. One day when the sun was scorching hot and the reflection of it in the water was blinding, I took my father to the mainland, in the Captain's boat.

"It looks like a squall," he said. "Better tie the boat up at the wharf. You'll need to spread the awning or the sun will roast you. I'll only be a couple of hours. Don't leave."

While I waited for him a captain's gig pulled in alongside. It was from a British ship–the sailors were in uniform. There were four apprentices rowing and a Mate steering. The Mate went ashore after telling the others to stay with the boat.

At that time Canadian ordinary seamen did not wear uniforms. The Britishers looked at my rough trousers and cotton shirt and looked away. They tied up their boat and sat down along the thwarts.

Presently rising clouds shut out the daylight and violent gusts of wind swept across the wharf blinding us with dust. After the wind came several vivid flashes of lightning, followed by deafening claps of thunder. All but one of the English boys ran for cover to a shipbuilder's store. The remaining boy looked frightened. He shouted to me, "Have you ever seen anything like this before?" I had begun to bail.

I was in no mood to spare his feelings. "Often," I shouted back. "And sometimes there's a water spout that sucks the harbour dry. Then it rains so hard that the hole fills up again before the ocean has a chance to come in. And boats like yours are swept right out to sea."

The rain lessened. The boys rejoined their companion. But here a violent eddy of wind swirled over us and down. One boy still on the wharf pulled on the painter and the others clung first to the boat's side and then to the stringer planks until helped from the water.

The lads were safe but the boat fittings, including the oars and a beautifully carved back-board, were floating out to sea.

The back-board of a captain's gig is an important piece of a ship's equipment. It is usually made of 1 1/2-inch teakwood or mahogany and is shaped to form the back of the seat which the captain occupies. The board is carved, bearing the design of the House flag, the coat-of arms, and the ship's name. Its origin may have been the "throne" in the old state barges of ancient Egypt and Rome. Sometimes it was handsomely decorated with an artistic design as well.

In an attack of any sort by enemy or storm, the back-board was the first article to be guarded by the crew.

The British must have seen the back-board afloat and feared the worst for a second gig arrived to investigate.

The rain ceased, and relieved of my bailing, I raised the awning to watch what was going on. As I climbed on the wharf, I was drenched, but when my father appeared he was not only dripping but covered with mud as well.

"We can't stay in these wet clothes," he said, "and I have a lot more business to do. Bring the gear and we'll leave it with the storekeeper. He'll find a boy to watch the boat. We'll get a room at that hotel over there. We both need a rub down and time to dry our clothes. That means overnight. You're wondering what happened to me? When we get things arranged, I'll tell you."

Safe in the hotel we were lying nude in our beds with mats below and above us and the mosquito netting well tucked in. The hotel porter had taken away our clothes to dry them and had provided us with steaming mugs of Brazilian coffee. We were comfortable and warm.

My father then told me of his own adventure. He had started down from Rio in a mule-drawn street car and had been caught in the squall. The car had no sides and rain slashed over everyone. Finally he got off and hailed a cab but soon the water in the streets was so deep that the mule refused to go. The door of the cab blew off its hinges in the gale. The windows were only curtained with some flimsy material, therefore the rain beat in by three openings. My father had to walk through a foot and a half of water along muddy streets.

Coming the other way were two small Brazilian children crying as they tried to keep their footing, a boy and a girl, evidently of one family.

"They weren't more than two or three years old and could have drowned," my father said. "I had no choice but to carry both of them the way they were heading. The older one, a boy, directed me down a side street. It was running with water too, and a young woman was splashing through it obviously coming to find them. Tears were running down her cheeks. She took the children in her arms somehow, and thanked me in Spanish, kissing me on both cheeks before leaving."

The next morning, in dry clothes though much soiled, we made our way to the boat and I waited there while my father transacted the remainder of his business.

The English boys and their Mate had spent the night with the storekeeper. They rowed off about noon, thankfully, I am sure, although minus their back-board, which we learned later was rescued by a market boat and returned to their ship.

We were moored about two miles out of port and when the doctor came on board for inspection he gave us a clean bill of health but warned us of the two diseases then prevalent, and the inadvisability of allowing anyone to go on shore who did not require to go. "No shore leave" was the order given to our crew and there was grumbling on all sides. Also my father warned everyone that it would be dangerous to buy fruit or food of any sort from the bumboats or market boats which come alongside when vessels are in port.

It was very hot on board, especially in the fo'c'sle where we slept. And at night, although told not to do so, some of us took our blankets and pillows aft on deck to cool off. I did this on the first night after the *Erin's Isle* was piloted into the port.

While lying unseen in the shadow of the fo'c'sle, I heard someone whistling and two of our men leaned over the rail, talking with someone alongside. Presently they put a rope over the rail and a man came on board. I could hear sound which indicated that drinking was going on and then all three men disappeared.

I got up then and found the rope firmly tied to the rail and dangling down the ship's side. I heard the soft swish of oars.

I knew what had happened but there was a watchman on duty and as an ordinary seaman it was not my business to report on the misbehaviour of anyone. Two of our crew had gone ashore, disobeying my father's orders, but they were gone and would be found out. Perhaps we would never see them again. It could be that they had deserted their ship.

Deserting was common to many busy ports and especially to Rio where shanghaiing was big business. Boarding-house masters engaged underworld characters to render sailors senseless by alcohol and drugs, sailors who came on shore and provided captains in need of additional crew with these helpless fellows for a price. They were taken on board unconscious and when they regained their senses found themselves far out to sea.

We lost four of our crew at Rio in this manner. Captains had no choice but to deal with these boarding-house masters. Crew had to be found or ships could not proceed on their way. In some cases the men called "crimps" hired by the masters would slug their victims if they couldn't gain control of them in any other way.

When we left Rio we had three new crew members. Although some of the sailors had gone ashore, none who did so contracted the fever except myself. I recovered quickly after we got out to sea, but our deck boy who had kept to the ship was taken with it seriously shortly after we came into port. He was removed then to an isolation hospital, where he died a week later.

From Rio we set sail for Albany, Australia, where we loaded Karri wood for London, England.

Disaster again deprived us of a crew member. Donovan was an Irish lad whom we all liked. He had a fine tenor voice and often entertained the rest of us off watch with Irish love songs which were a favourite with him. He had a colleen waiting for him in Belfast and they were to be married when we reached London, where she planned to meet him. But one night when Donovan went aloft to reave the gantling while I stood watching, there was a shout and I was knocked 10 feet along the deck. When I regained consciousness, Donovan was being carried on a canvas stretcher to the main hatch. All were silent as he was covered with the Ensign.

"You barely escaped being killed yourself, lad." It was my father speaking. I knew this to be true but I could think only of my shipmate whose dreams of happiness would never be realized.

# The Stormy South Pacific

Many early books about adventures at sea in sailing ships are considered by adults, at least, to be the product of some writer's imagination. But most of these, if not true, could indeed have been true. Castaways, such as Robinson Crusoe, and stowaways, there have been. I would say there always will be.

In my day, after Cape Horn was rounded to westward, the stormy Southern Pacific challenged seamen's skill. To sail a safe course, to escape shipwreck on some one of the many rocky islands, often kept all hands ready for days and for nights. If they slept, they did so with ears trained to hear commands and one eye open.

I was Captain of the *Elginshire* when we first saw the famous Pitcairn Island.

From a distance of fifty miles it looked harmless enough—a green island and a small but rather high one, like a mossy bank. When we sailed on we found the bank to be a rocky coastline, a thousand feet above sea level at its highest point, a precipice overgrown with vegetation. As we passed near we saw Bounty Bay on the north-west with many steps up the rocky cliffs leading to the only settlement on the island. We imagined there might be a hundred or more inhabitants. There were boat houses on the beach and a number of long canoe-like boats moored there. The roofs of the houses were of metal, probably iron, and ridged so that when rain fell it ran down into troughs and from there into barrel-like containers. There was no other drinking water on lonely Pitcairn.

The breakers were tossing white foam up the steep cliffs and we all realized what a terrific courage must have possessed the hearts of the mutineers who had taken refuge there so many years before. This they did after setting adrift Captain Bligh whose treatment of them had been unbearably cruel. It is recorded that one of the mutineers, Fletcher Christian, had read of the existence of this island and so guided the *Bounty* there after the mutiny.

The people in the small settlement on Pitcairn were said to have formed a co-operative and to be very contented.

Pitcairn was only one of many islands which we saw and passed by without visiting. We had a cargo to deliver at Sydney, Australia, and there was not time for exploring on that trip.

The South Pacific was an awesome stretch of water and its islands varied from ideal locations for easy living, such as Tahiti, to groups mountainous and uninhabited. Ships running the easting down to Australia kept a watch for a group with sheer rocky sides known as the Crozet. These islands were mere piles of rock with practically no vegetation and inhabited only by birds, among them the albatross. They were attacked by walls of water and have been responsible for many shipwrecks. A ship as far as half a mile away on the windward side can feel a tremor when the towering waves strike the Crozet rocks.

The islands lie between Australia and South Africa but nearer to Africa.

Our destination was Sydney and while there we learned more about the Crozet Islands. Freemantle is on the west coast of Australia. Here, on the beaches, children loved to play. One day a boy whose father was a fisherman, was putting out with him to sea when they noticed a large bird lying on its side in the water. A wire was fastened around its neck and threaded through a small slab of wood. When the half dead bird, an albatross, was removed from the water, the wooden slab was found to be carved with a few words in the French language.

The fisherman who happened to be French, was able to read the inscription, at least in part. The word "Crozet" was clear and "pour l'amour de Dieu."

Placing the dying albatross in the boat, he drew the boat up on the beach leaving the boy to watch it while he cut the wire and hurried away with the slab of wood to a naval post. He learned that a French ship, the *Tamaris*, had indeed been wrecked and lost near the Crozet group only a month before.

But owing to a dispute as to which country, Australia or France, should attempt to rescue those of the *Tamaris'* crew who might still be alive, aid was not sent for almost three months. Then, in December, the *Martha*, a French warship, set out with provisions, clothing and medical supplies.

But the poor wretches who waited ran out of food and water and somehow managed to get to another island in the group, no doubt hoping to find a cache of food known to be there. The *Martha* returned without achieving a rescue and reported that all of the thirteen castaways were presumed dead.

When the *Elginshire* sailed past the Crozet Islands, I thought of the men whose bleached bones were probably somewhere among the piles of rock. We were at least half a mile away and thankful to be as night was falling. I couldn't see the islands but I knew we were in their vicinity, for there was a change in the direction of the waves which affected the movement of the ship. It was undoubtedly the effect of a backwash from cliffs.

Immediately I hurried on deck and shouted for all hands. I ordered the helm up.

A terrific storm was shaping up and we were receiving the backwash from the not far distant Crozet rocks. The *Elginshire* began to heel and the boys had to climb to the fife-rails, the water was so deep on deck. The topsails lowered, we brought her as far around as we dared.

We bowled past the dangerous group with only a margin of safety. We knew this when the water on deck receded and the rhythm of our ship's motion became normal. It was a pitch-black night. We could not see the outline of the islands, only the high white spray which reminded us of our peril had we approached too near.

In the roar of the wind and water I had imagined that I heard the howl of a dog. I did not mention this to the men because some superstitious people believe that the sound is the precedent of someone's death. But at dawn as we slowed our speed and gathered at the stern for a look back at the menacing Crozet, I saw a piece of wreckage like the splintered shaft of a main mast floating as if toward us, impelled by the will of a black-and-white dog clinging desperately to it.

"A dog out there," cried Bowlby, our Second Mate. "He was howling last night. We've got to save him."

I smiled to Bowlby. "You heard him too?" I said.

"I was afraid to tell anybody," he admitted. "I thought— you know what, sir. How can we get him, sir? Poor devil, he's had a night of it."

The sea was now relatively calm for that region, or so it seemed to us after the night of storm.

"Lower the gig," I ordered the two eager-looking apprentices.

"*You're* not going, sir?" It was the First Mate objecting.

But I scarcely had time to inform him for the two young men were already carrying out my instructions.

"Yes, I'm going," I said. It was a tricky operation but not a dangerous one and it was successful.

We called our new crew member "Crozie." He was a beautiful black-and-white American spaniel and he accompanied us on our next voyage around the world.

His owners and their ship were undoubtedly victims of a cruel storm at sea.

A year later when we put into New York harbour, Crozie was still with us. I consulted the authorities but in the list of American ships missing there was no record of one having been lost about the time we passed the most threatening pile of rock I was ever to see in mid-ocean.

Crozie was by nature a landlubber. I found him a kind mistress in the person of an English woman who kept a boarding home for sailors near the docks. We missed him but our next voyage would take us around the Cape and during storms encountered while he journeyed with us the spaniel had been susceptible to seasickness. It was kinder to leave him on land.

In the exciting days when sailing ships were queens of the sea, men who preferred a sailor's life to the less eventful if safer life on terra firma knew well the risks they were taking. To be swept overboard, to be left as part of a wreckage on a lonely island, were fates common enough. With all they owned swept away, with no food nor shelter they took refuge behind rocks or in trees, ate what was edible of plants, fruit and fish, if the latter could be caught. If lucky enough to have saved firearms, they could shoot wild birds and animals. In a state of desperate doubt they watched for signs of vessels on the horizon. From tree tops or rocky ledges near shore, day after day, they hoped and prayed, signalling, sometimes in vain as ships sped from sight unaware of their silent messages and their plight.

If several were spared death they sometimes took up residence, forming a tiny colony, building homes of whatever material they had with which to build, and settling down for months, even years, but never quite abandoning the hope of rescue.

In the middle eighteen hundreds about three-quarters of the sailing ships loading in English ports for Australia were Canadian built ships, but although they were in the majority, the American built ships could out-strip them in speed. American ships were some of the fastest ships ever to sail the deep. The fastest one of all for long distance voyaging was called *The Sovereign of the Seas*. But for one day of sailing another American ship *The Lightning* outstripped even the *Sovereign* by twelve miles.

The *Sovereign* in 24 hours sailed 424 miles: the *Lightning* in 24 hours, 436 miles.

But I am proud to record that a number of Canadian ships

were fast in sail, too. Perhaps the most famous of these was the *Marco Polo*, which I have mentioned elsewhere. She won world acclaim by making a return trip from Liverpool to Australia in five months and two days. A one-way voyage before that astonishing sail was estimated to take at least four months. "White wings–they never grow weary. . . ."*

* From an old song

# Chills and Thrills in Chile

Our ship, the *Elginshire*, was in Talcahuano loading grain for England. It was Easter time when nowadays everyone dashes away in a car to spend a weekend, or takes a rail or bus trip.

A boat trip was available to us at Talcahuano–in our own boat ship-to-shore. To go to the nearby city and see processions was nothing much different from home town stuff, like the sights to be seen in ten thousand cities. What was the use of being down at the southern tip of South America and seeing only what we could see at home?

Boat trips were a thrill for us when we were at out-of-the-way ports. Our purpose was to see unfamiliar country and to study the people of that country. Also these trips provided a complete change for the crew from ship routine. I was the skipper and the apprentices whom I took with me were from sixteen to eighteen years of age. I included the acting Third Mate, who was nineteen.

On such trips all regulations as to the relation of apprentices to master were suspended, with the exception of one–that I was at all times responsible for their safety. This suspension gave me a chance to act as undignified as I liked–much as Dads and Uncles do with boys at a summer camp or on a holiday. But I had to be on the alert at all times for possible emergencies.

I went on shore first and attended to business connected with the ship, for offices were closing at noon for the weekend. The gig was at the wharf waiting for me when I had finished. I stepped in. The Third Mate, Vennan, and Newsome, the elder apprentice, rowed me back to the ship.

As I got out of the gig onto the gangway platform, I said to Vennan, "Drop the gig astern, and after you get your dinner, have Newsome, Grey, Davy, and ordinary seaman Pelan help you to get the port lifeboat into the water and rigged up."

Their faces immediately brightened. "While you are doing that," I continued, "I'll have the steward get the grub together and I'll collect the rest of the things we need for fishing, exploring, and emergencies."

There was plenty to do. We had to find boards that would fit into the lifeboat to sleep on both in the thwarts and on the bottom. Also, we packed kits with what might be needed if anything should happen, from the sail to the boat herself. Although the distances to the places where we planned to go were not so very far, only some 20 miles, many things unforeseen could occur.

Most of our trip was along the coast where there was ocean to the west of us for 10,000 miles, and if a sudden gale sprang up, well, we were too near a rock-bound coast for safety. The worst could happen easily, the end of the boat and of us, too.

We all got quite a thrill as we prepared ourselves and the boat for a trip to a place where it was possible that no one had landed since the time of Drake, or Anson, or perhaps Darwin.

Now the lifeboat was built to carry 28 men as well as the usual lifeboat equipment—oars, masts, sails, compass, hatchets and other tools, and, of course, provisions.

It was seven o'clock in the evening before we were ready to set out. When I slid down the tackle and took my place at the tiller, I could hardly believe my senses: the boat was loaded almost to the gunwales, and there was hardly room for anyone to move in her. It looked as if we were setting out on a voyage around the world.

But there would be time enough for rearranging space for

rowing, etc., when we needed it. There was a gentle breeze and a fair wind as we prepared to set off. I checked over our crew. Everyone was in his place.

"All aboard," I shouted. "Cast off and hoist the mainsail."

I noted the time again: 7:15 p.m., Thursday, April the eighth.

The loaded boat and her crew slipped noiselessly down the bay towards the vast and stormy southern ocean. We moved along in silence for quite a time. No one seemed to want to talk. We were each dreaming our own dreams as to what might come in the way of adventure. Near the rocky island of Quiriquima, which guards the entrance to Talcahuano Harbour, the winds dropped light. Soon it was calm and the boat motionless.

Vennan said to me, "Shall we get the oars out?"

"No," I replied. "Too much trouble now to shift a lot of this junk, and there is no hurry. We'll anchor so we will drift if the tide's running flood."

Vennan called to Davy, "You and Grey clear the anchor and the anchor rope, and drop the anchor over soon as you're ready."

In a moment or two there was a splash and the sound of the swiftly running rope. When the anchor hit bottom, the rope slowed up and Davy grabbed it.

"Wait till you see how it leads," I ordered, "then give her another five fathoms and make fast."

This was done.

Again silence, except for a very faint rippling sound as the tide flowed by. I began to think, "Why so much silence?" when Pelan from the midship thwart answered my unspoken question. "Gee, it's getting cold."

"That's it Pelan," I said. "We're in for a change of weather. It's coming on foggy. Dig out those oilskins for you're going to need them. Vennan can get his and mine. They are in the stern locker."

We all struggled into the more or less sticky oilskin coats and wiggled ourselves into the most comfortable position for resting. I dozed off for a few minutes but a sudden movement brought me full awake. It was the main sheet moving across my body. A stiff breeze had come up. "Come on, boys," I shouted. "Fair wind, a fine southerly wind. Up with the anchor before she over-runs it."

A few minutes "Yo-hoing" and Davy called, "Anchors away."

I felt the boat respond, and gather way with the freshening breeze. There was still dense fog but very low over the water. Above was blue sky and a brilliant moon. It was now after 11 p.m. We sped on our course in silence again, broken only by the rippling water from the bow and the musical gurgle in the wake.

At 2 a.m. (Good Friday morning), the fog cleared. We checked our position. We had made a good course. At 3:40 we were off Penca Point at the entrance to Talcahuano Bay. Here the breeze fell away again to a calm, and in brilliant moonlight we set to work to rearrange the stuff and to place the bunk boards, so that some of us could get a little sleep. After the boards were arranged, an oar was lashed horizontally between two masts at about three feet above the gunwale. The sails were lowered and spread across this ridge pole and lashed out to the gunwales, making a very comfortable looking tent.

The hurricane lamp was lit and hung from the ridge-pole. We were now much warmer. Four crawled into the bunks. Pelan with all his oilskins on sat forward with his back against the mast, keeping watch.

I curled up on the stern sheets, and with overcoat, and oilskin coat on top, with a blanket for a pillow, felt very comfortable. But before I did this, by the light of the lantern, I wrote up our log, recording the trip times, the distances and the weather, just as it would later appear in the ship's log. Before Vennan settled himself, I asked him to bait and set one of our big fishing lines such as those used for cod or snapper. I told Pelan to watch it.

A few minutes later both Vennan and I were asleep.

Again I was startled awake. Pelan was standing beside me on the stern sheets struggling with the fishing line. He gave a shout.

I sat up, to be knocked down by a huge squirming marine creature that had hit me in the chest. I jumped to my feet only to have them pushed from under me by the threshing creature now in the bottom of the boat. As I tried to get up, I yelled to no one in particular, "The darn thing looks like a water snake. They're more poisonous than a rattle snake."

"I'll jump on it," Pelan cried. "I have on my sea boots. He can't bite me through them."

"Wait a second," I commanded. "Here's the tiller. Hit him with that."

But I spoke too confidently. The tiller was wedged. I couldn't get it off.

"Never mind," Pelan called. "I've got one of the boat hatchets."

As Pelan struck at the thing, there came a wild yell from Grey, who with Davy was in the bottom bunk, but now sitting up with both hands around one of his booted feet. "He's cut my toe off," he screamed, following his cry with moans of pain.

Davy roared at him. "The thing is coming this way. Get off those boards will you, so I can get up!"

The Third Mate crawled forward off the boards and seized the boat hook. Davy had good reason to yell. The creature had passed over him and gone forward. Then the Third Mate, getting a glimpse in the moonlight, let drive the boat hook into its head which pinned it down. There was a failing attempt by the wounded thing to pull free while Vennan held it where it was with the hook and shouted for the hatchet. Newsome, who had the hatchet in his hand went to Vennan's aid and cut off the head of the captive, which Vennan then held aloft on the boat hook where we could get a look at it.

It was an enormous female conger eel, about 6 feet long. Its great eyes stared at us even in death. Its snake-like body was silver-coloured.

The excitement was now over, but no one felt like sleeping.

It was coming daylight and we were glad that the night was over.

Davy sat on the thwart groping for his boots. "Gosh, the boat's sprung a leak!" he exclaimed. He grabbed his blanket off the bottom. "I can see right through and the water's coming in."

The deepest water in the South Pacific is along the Chile Coast. There, more than any other place in the world, the coastline takes a beating from the sea. Big rollers had begun to come in while we undertook to master the conger eel. We cut it up hurriedly to make way for more important matters—the leak in our boat which might prove serious if not immediately attended to.

Looking down from where I stood by the mainmast, I could see the damage. "You're a prize harpooner alright," I snapped at Vennan. "Grey, jamb a rag into the hole until I get the gear to patch it."

Grey swiftly took off his boot and used his own sock to stop the bubble of water. I reached in the locker for my repair box and found a piece of heavily white-leaded canvas which fitted securely over the hole. The boat was now water-tight again.

"Go aft, Newsome, and bail her out." I said. "And now that the sun is up, we may as well get on with our voyage. Vennan and Davy, get the anchor up. The rest of us will take down the tent and hoist the sails out of the way and ready for the breeze."

Everyone set to work.

"I'll take the stroke bar," I said. "We'll row along the shore-line to the first bay. Watch for a landing place free from rocks and surf."

We found the bay, alright, but in the whole length of it there was no safe landing.

I gave over my oar to Vennan now and took his place at the tiller while Newsome and Pelan bent to the other two oars, but hardly had we exchanged places when we noted a breeze approaching along the water and in a moment or two it was up with us—a fine north-west wind.

"Unship the oars, boys," I called, "and keep your eyes peeled for a landing place."

We had almost despaired of seeing one as we were near the end of the bay and did not want to go on to a distant one until the next day. Then a small bend in the shore at the southern part formed a tiny cove, and in it we found a short piece of sandy beach. At last!

I rounded the boat to and Davy cast over the anchor, while the others dropped the sails. As soon as she swung, we backed her in with two oars, while Newsome with the stern rope in his hand, got ready to jump onto one of the boulders. Safely there, he picked his way ashore without bringing the boat into a striking distance of the bottom—there was quite a bit of surf. As Newsome jumped, Davy checked her with the anchor rope, and we then unshipped the oars.

All around us were submerged boulders and kelp except for one narrow clear channel where we would be able to pull the boat ashore. After close inspection we proceeded.

"Make fast the anchor rope," I called to Davy, and to Newsome, "Make fast the stern-line to that old timber there in the sand."

This was done.

"Now," I ordered, "let's get the cooking utensils and grub ashore, not forgetting the conger. Just catch a turn with that stern-line, Newsome, and stand by to slack the boat out to her anchor, as soon as we get the stuff out of her."

The stern of the boat was now being held in about two and one half feet of water. Davy, Pelan and Grey jumped out and proceeded to carry the things ashore as Vennan and I passed these to them. We then waded in, while I called to Newsome, "Let go that stern-line by the run." This allowed the boat to move well out.

Davy and Pelan became self-appointed cooks. Davy asked, "Anybody want conger?"

We all had a good look. Nobody spoke.

"Say something, somebody," Davy urged. "Lots of people eat

conger." Newsome turned down his thumb and Pelan and Vennan did likewise.

"So," said Davy, "it's corned beef and fried potatoes, is it? We'll use the eel for bait."

Breakfast over, Vennan, Newsome and I went north to the point between the cove and the bay to do some fishing and to explore generally, while the others took their turn at cleaning up before going south to do as we were planning to do.

I called to them, "It may be late afternoon before we are back. We'll make dinner and tea one meal. Better take the grub box. We've got some hard biscuits and cheese. Don't forget a bottle of water."

Fishing was poor for us. Although we cast out a couple of lines, we caught only one rock cod each. But it was very comfortable in the sun on the rocks and after looking around for shells and crabs in the sandy spots, we lay in the sun, not without our clothing as some sun bathers have a habit of doing. But the warmth penetrated what we wore and we were soon fast asleep after our rather disturbed night.

We woke about four and had dinner and tea, as planned. I then suggested that we get back before dark because I wanted to examine some old timbers which we had seen sticking out of the water beyond a sharp ledge of rock.

When we arrived, we found Davy and Pelan already revealing their curiosity about these timbers—they were pieces of wreckage. "Get anything?" I said to no one in particular.

"Yes," Pelan answered. "We got three small rock cod. We saw some large crabs and that kelp out there is just alive with octopus."

I knew that there were octopuses in Talcahuano at some seasons, and it was easy to believe that there were others along the coast. "How big?" I wanted to know.

"Three or four feet long," Pelan said, but Grey called out, "Bigger than that. Anyway, nobody had better wade or swim out among that kelp."

"Why not try to catch one?" Vennan suggested.

"Why not?" Newsome asked, and I echoed his words. "We have good bait with the conger, and remember Vennan is an excellent harpoonist. He damaged the conger and the boat at the same time."

"Davy, you have a try this time," Vennan urged.

While Newsome and Vennan proceeded to finish getting supper, I fixed up and set a line for the squid. With a generous piece of conger for bait, we might be lucky in getting one while having our meal.

Squid was now the topic of conversation and everyone planned that when the meal was over we would get into the boat and watch for them.

Squid or octopuses are eight-armed creatures with two rows of suckers on each arm. They feed on carrion and are especially fond of crabs. They were so plentiful along the south coast of England in 1900 that they were a plague to the shell-fish fisheries. They robbed lobster and crab pots, and had a fine time of it for a while. They did the same along the west coast of France.

An octopus with arms extended is usually about 3 or 4 feet in diameter, although there is a species which reaches 6 feet in diameter, but the body part of this fellow is only about one foot across.

When the octopus finds his prey, he wraps his arms around it. I have been asked if the creature will attack a man. We know that it has done so, but have not heard of a man being eaten by it. But if he were swimming and it attacked him, what chance would he have to escape from drowning, held perhaps below water or, if clinging to a rock, pinned there by this sea monster?

The octopus is more active by night. During the day it sleeps among shells or behind boulders which hide it from enemies.

Although the hook was baited with a generous piece of conger there was no evidence of pull on the line during supper hour.

As I picked up the stern line, while Grey and Davy were

giving me a hand with the boat before we settled to eat, I noted a hole that had been dug close by.

I questioned them.

"We were looking for gold, sir," Davy said teasingly, "and when we struck metal, then the sand really began to fly. But we soon discovered it was just a pile of loose chain – likely the chain locker of the vessel these old timbers belong to. Pretty old, anyway. We can see about that in the morning, before we leave. Gosh, this boat is hard to move through that thick kelp."

After the three of us had given a good pull and there was no movement, I said, "It's not the kelp or she'd move slowly. The boat has grounded on one of the boulders. The tide is falling. That's not so good. If the tide falls much," I warned, "and if the boulder is sharp, it will put a hole into the boat when the weight comes on it. If we pull too hard though, and drag her off it, she'll suffer just the same damage. However, she can't stay that way, and we can't go out to her either if that kelp is full of squid and crabs. Better, I guess, if we carefully try to pull her free. Perhaps it won't hurt her much. She has good planking. We'd have her on the beach then, anyway, and could patch her up."

I called to the others to help us which they did, while we walked up and down the beach in an effort to twist her a bit. Then I called, "Now all together, boys."

We had scarcely accomplished our task when Pelan shouted, "Look, look!" He pointed to seaward of the boat.

We stopped to stare with him.

"Heavens above," I muttered, "this will either be our salvation or the end of the boat and everything we have. That will mean walking 15 miles back over the mountains instead of rowing."

# More of Chile

What Pelan had seen seaward of the boat were a couple of low glassy swells. This was the beginning of a surf period. It might last only a few hours, or several days! The very first swell might finish the boat if it broke into her instead of seaward of her. This would fill her instead of lifting her.

"Here they come," yelled Vennan, and I yelled back, "Grab this rope and stand by. Pull as you never pulled before until you feel it slack. Then up the beach as if a crab 14 feet long were just behind you."

The first roller was rapidly coming into the more shallow water and piling higher and higher as it shortened, and as it felt the drag of the bottom. It was now some 6 or 7 feet higher than the boat—a long green glassy wall. The water on which our boat was grounded was drawing off the rock to meet it, and the boat began to tip drunkenly to seaward.

"Gee, boys," I cried, "she's going to slip seaward as well, and if she does, it's all up." I groaned. "Hold on to that line."

But just as we were sure that the almost vertical front on the roller was going to fall on the boat, it struck the kelp instead, flattened and slid under us as the kelp spread its far-reaching arms over the surface.

Our boat was free and up the beach we went with it until a sudden increase in drag told us that she was certainly on the beach.

"Hold her against the outgoing stream," I ordered, as the water ran back for the next breaker. Then grabbing each gunwale, we struggled farther up the beach as the second breaker surged around us to our waists. When the roller went back, the boat was high, dry, and safe. The third swell which followed was less high than the other two, and did not reach her. While the surf continued after that, none of the swells were as dangerous as the first two.

The anchor rope had slipped when we pulled on it, and the third swell lifted the boat which was lucky for us. We would be able to get the anchor when we launched. We were mighty lucky all round.

As we got our breath and realized that we might have been smashed to pieces instead of achieving a full rescue, I said, "I think we all deserve a good square meal. Let's hop to it."

We prepared to do so fairly leisurely, for we could not leave our location until the surf period was over. But we would not spend another night there. All agreed to that. The end of the surf period was likely to come soon enough for departure in daylight,

We did not bother making camp, but put up the tent again in the boat where we would catch some sleep if possible. But Vennan protested, "What about the squid we were going to catch?"

"Yes, what about it?" Newsome wanted to know.

"You're a good swimmer, Newsome," Pelan said gruffly. "You swim out with the bait and we'll stay here and pull in the catch for you from the beach."

But there was no squid fishing that night.

We had lit a fire which cast a flickering light over the beach. Vennan walked down toward the sea. The tide had gone down a lot and some of the kelp was lying in the wash. The rock which had threatened the boat for a while was now clearly above water.

Then there was a shout. It was Vennan. "The squid," he cried. "I stepped on one. Help!"

111

I grabbed the lantern and with the others rushed to Vennan's aid. Davy was ahead of me with the boat hook and Pelan with a hatchet. We could see nothing at first. Vennan too had vanished. Then we saw him. He was plunging around among the kelp with a four foot squid. In the low water they had the look of wrestlers.

Davy managed to drive the boat hook into the squid's body without harming Vennan, and it promptly let go its hold and wound itself around the hook instead. Meanwhile, the rest of us helped Vennan get a foothold among the slippery kelp and to the dry beach, where we set him down, unhurt but badly frightened.

When he got his breath, he said, "Talk about hunting squid. They are hunting us. I saw about five or six slipping through that kelp into the sea."

The rest of the boys helped Davy drag the captured one up onto the dry sand. We examined it. It was almost dead but its arms kept coiling and uncoiling in a way that made us shiver while its huge eyes shone like the lenses of auto headlights.

We killed the thing properly and then prepared to turn in. We were all glad that we had decided to sleep in the boat and not on the beach. Squid are really helpless out of water or beyond it on the wet kelp. Nevertheless, we were on the alert.

"We'll keep watch," I said, "and stay where we are until morning. We'll take one and a half hours each, and keep the rifle handy."

In about 15 minutes we were all asleep except Vennan on watch.

At 4:30, Vennan called me. "It's your watch, sir," he said. After a few minutes during which I got the sleep out of my eyes, I asked him, "Have you seen anything?"

"No," he said. "I haven't and don't want to. After the moon got up I thought I saw all kinds of things around that wreck and out by the kelp."

I smiled at him. "Time you turned in," I said. "I'll call all hands at six. Where's the rifle?"

He handed it to me.

The moon was still making queer patterns on the sand, like huge crabs when the tiny clouds created shadows as they passed across. I looked at the old ship and wondered what she had been. There might be treasure hidden under that chain. I decided that we would dig some more in the morning before leaving her.

Then something moved in the place where the boys had been digging. What on earth was that? It couldn't be alive, but it was. I gave a gasp as a pair of eyes shone at me above the hole. I shouted and let go with the rifle in their general direction.

Everyone was up like a flash.

"What was it? What was it?" they wanted to know.

"Darned if I can tell you," I said. "It came out of the place you dug into."

"Out of the hole?" Davy whispered. "Gee, I'm glad daylight's coming."

"When the sun is up we'll investigate," I said.

We were a silent bunch, I'll admit, for the next 15 or 20 minutes. Then as the light strengthened, Vennan said, "I don't much mind fights with something I can see, even an octopus, but I don't want to fool with things that I can't see."

"It's light enough, now, boys," I told them. "Everybody grab a weapon – hatchet, boat hook, anything, and Vennan bring the other rifle."

We left the boat and began to approach the wreck cautiously. As we did so we saw nothing. Finally we came close enough to look into the small excavation. Nothing was there. We breathed more freely. But on closer examination we found foot prints. They were of a hoofed animal which had been digging. What for? we all wondered.

"Well, that's better than a ghost," I said. "But what on earth was it and what was it digging for?"

Rather disappointed, we went back to our boat and prepared to get it on skids for launching. The surf was over. We agreed not to wait for breakfast, but to move on to Dichato Bay further along the coast. As we worked, Newsome whispered, "I see something in the bushes at the top of the sand ridge behind the wreck. Still, everybody."

We obeyed him, and looked closely. Two native children were looking through the bushes at us. We dashed up the beach and they ran yelling among the trees but we got to the top in time to have a closer view. From the ridge we could see a native hut about a quarter of a mile back. "Humans," I said, relieved. "Let's leave the boat and have some breakfast. We may see more of interest here."

We built up our fire and cooked a good meal. After breakfast we cleared up while Newsome was on watch. We left him there and set out to investigate where we had seen the hut.

As we approached we noted that there were several huts. After about ten minutes walk through scrub and grass we came to the first one. This proved to be a part of the native village of Culimo. Two men with their women came out to meet us. They looked friendly, as most people in foreign countries where I have been have looked to me. They could speak no English and we could not understand the kind of Spanish which they used, although I knew a little of that commonly spoken in the cities. I would try to make myself understood anyway because we wanted to buy some food.

The older woman got the hang of my attempt and dashed behind the hut, bringing out a squawking skinny chicken and a couple of long thin loaves of what they call bread. *"Quantō?"* I asked her. *"Cinco pesetas,"* she replied. "You know how to charge if nothing else," I muttered. (The price to us was about twice as much as we would have paid in Talcahuano.)

Then the other woman came out with an even skinnier chicken. I shook my head. The words came to me, *"Esto basta, gracias señora."* I was pleased when she came back with, *"Muy bien."* She actually understood my Spanish.

We were satisfied, now, that these people were not unfriendly, and certainly not supernatural. We went back to the boat with our skinny chicken and two loaves, waving to them while they waved to us. A half dozen small children trailed after us, getting farther and farther astern of us as we neared camp.

We did have fried chicken but I think it must have climbed the Andes every morning of its life. However, with our sharp knives we managed to cut bites from it. But the bread was more of a problem. It needed even harsher treatment. It made our hard sea biscuits seem soft by comparison. However, it was surprising what a good hammer and hot coffee did to it; and with our appetites what they were, it tasted mighty good.

Breakfast over, we all set to work to launch the boat. A fresh northerly wind and choppy sea only made us more anxious to be off. Everyone worked at high pressure, tossing everything that was movable out to lighten her, then working a board under the keel to slide her down to the water more easily. Davy got aboard and pulled in on the anchor rope and held her with the stern rope to keep her steady. After she was launched, we had everything aboard in a few minutes of quick effort, sails up, the anchor up, and we were away before a splendid fair wind to our real destination, Dichato Bay. There was no more thought of seeking after squid or old wrecks now. Teasingly I mentioned doing so to the boys and received the unanimous answer, "No, sir. Maybe next time."

By eleven o'clock that morning, we were at anchor in our chosen spot in Dichato Bay, a sheltered cove where the sea was as smooth as a pond. We backed the boat in as before, but due to the smooth sea, we let her ground and then passed everything ashore, mast, sails, and all except two oars which we left for Newsome and Pelan. They went on a hundred yards or so to the mouth of a small creek which formed a natural slipway. We walked to this place and waited for them. We then pulled the boat high and dry up the bank of the creek, moored her securely to a nearby tree, and then set about building a camp.

With spades which we had brought, we dug a large square hole in the sand—it was really only three-sided, for the side towards the sea was low with the appearance of an open basement. We covered the floor with several thicknesses of fir-like branches. With masts and oars across the top of the hole and sails spread over these, it looked mighty comfortable. It certainly was not water tight, but we saw no indication of rain.

If it did blow up a rainstorm, we would have to put more slant to the roof and move closer together.

While we were building the camp, Davy and Pelan were getting lunch ready. When lunch was over, it was 5 p.m.

We had seen a large house about half a mile back with trees around it. We left Grey to watch camp and the rest of us set off for the house where we hoped to buy more provisions. The only weapon we took was the rifle I carried.

As we neared the house, a dozen large dogs came out barking loudly. I was glad that I had the rifle, but they were quite friendly. Their barking speedily brought their master to view—a Chilean of about forty and wearing the typical poncho, a blanket with a hole in the middle through which the head is thrust. He greeted us pleasantly in Spanish, speaking slowly and clearly. I quite readily understood his *"Buenos dias Señor. Entre,"* and even his *"De donde ha venido usted?"*

After returning his welcome in Spanish, with the aid of my little Spanish dictionary and conversation book (which I was never without), I managed to tell him that we would like to buy some chickens. Also, seeing an orchard beside the house, I included a request for some fruit. I explained that we were sailors and that our ship was in Talcahuano, adding that we were on a holiday trip.

After I had struggled through these bits of information, he said, *"Venga por aqui,"* or, "Come along this way."

We did so.

His name, he said, was Pantelon Reys, and this was his ranch.

He took us into the house which was Spanish in style but with quite a few American features. From there we went into the orchard where he told us to help ourselves. There was a great variety of fruit, but only some were ripe at that time. We helped ourselves to lemons, oranges, peaches, pears and quince.

Presently Pantelon called his dogs and gave them orders. With a lot of yelping they rushed off into the bush. In less than a quarter hour, they returned with little barks of satisfaction, driving a wild pig before them. Our host quickly trained his revolver on the pig, shooting it through the head. We recalled the tracks we had found in the sand by the wreck. This was obviously.a domestic pig gone wild, which had become a scavenger. Another mystery had been solved for us.

While we were gathering the plentiful fruit, the Chilean asked if we would like to sleep in his house. I tried to be polite, explaining that we really preferred to sleep in a tent or in the open. He shook his head over my admission that we wished to sleep outside when there were good beds available. Probably he put it down to another foolish idea of the *"Gringos,"* for he shrugged his shoulders.

From the house, assisted by a servant, he brought us eggs, milk and fowl. When we left we were loaded with gifts from his larder as well as from the orchard. We had intended to buy but he refused to accept anything from us. We all spoke sincerely our *"Muchas gracias,"* and *"Buenas noches"* in varying pronunciation.

We trailed off toward camp.

Grey, whom we had left on watch, waved as he saw us coming. "Well you certainly missed an interesting experience, Grey," I said, "but at least we've brought you something good to eat."

Davy and Vennan prepared a meal which included fried eggs and an abundance of fruit.

The supper over, we settled to sleep. Although the boat was perfectly safe as to weather, we knew that she might prove a big temptation if caught sight of by Chilean fishermen. Therefore, while the rest of us slept in our camp, one-and-a-half-hour watches were kept as before. The one on watch held a Winchester across his knees. But nothing happened to distress us. Most of us reported seeing the shadows of moving animals after the moon came by, but we remembered the wild pig and did not stir to investigate.

At 6 a.m. it was "all hands" and breakfast. And what a breakfast for Easter! No one could have had a better one – with fresh fruit, fried chicken, and then stewed fruit, biscuits and coffee.

It was one magnificent morning, bright and clear and nippy, much like October in Canada. We lay around the campfire after our hearty meal and dozed in our blankets. It was ten o'clock or mid-morning before we bestirred ourselves and launched our boat, pulled on the gear and rigged her up. By noon we were on our way to the little village named after the bay at the southern end of Dichato.

Here we landed and made friends with some natives by means of our elementary Spanish. These natives were quite primitive. They lived in small huts and used wooden ploughs. They also used oxen and ox carts. The children were intelligent and bright looking. They seemed to understand us much better than the grown-ups, and when I showed the older ones my Spanish conversation book, I found that they could read. Their parents could not do so.

Because it was smooth in the bay we only anchored the boat, and pulled her stern right to the beach. After spending a few interesting hours, we said farewell to Dichato. We had to be back for work at our ship in the morning and we might run into calms or storms. In choosing the time for departing, we had to take these things into consideration.

About 8 p.m. we were off under all sail with a strengthening breeze and an increasing sea. We left further encounters with squid and the investigation of wrecks for another voyage.

As we came toward Penca Point and the re-entrance to the harbour, the swell was rapidly mounting and steering became more and more difficult. We were experiencing the thrills of a roller-coaster as the boat slid down the faces of these southern ocean swells. The freshening wind was bringing foam to their crests and dusk was falling. We were glad to round the point and get into the harbour out of their reach.

We had been sailing along a rockbound coast; we were thankful for the safety which the harbour afforded. In its choppy sea, and with a strong leading breeze, we sped up the bay throwing spray over everything, but as we neared the ship the wind fell away. By the time we ran alongside our good old packet, storms and threatening seas were forgotten. It was good to be back for it was now growing dark.

The watchman threw us a rope and we pulled along under the tackles, clambered up the pilot ladder, left Pelan and Newsome to look to the tackles, mustered all hands, hoisted the boat to the rail, triced her in and that was the end of our Easter voyage of adventure. It remained only to take out our gear from the boat and our additional grub. Then, with some steaming hot coffee from the galley, and some of the cook's hot cross buns, we ate our supper. As Eight Bells was struck we sought our respective bunks to dream of wrecks and phantom pigs, conger eels and squid.

# A Cat and a Turtle Go to Sea

One of the finest wooden ships ever built in the Maritimes was the *Erin's Isle*, a three-masted, full-rigged, three sky-sail yard ship. She was rigged the same as many of the famous clipper ships of earlier days which established the prestige of Canadian shipbuilders and seamen the world over. I was very proud of this ship. I was the Mate.

The *Erin's Isle* lay in the docks at Cardiff, Wales, loading coal for Rio de Janeiro, Brazil. Along the docks on the town side ran dozens and dozens of pairs of rails, such as you see in our great freight terminals here. Some of the other ships moored there that evening were also loading. As the cars of coal were hoisted and tipped, clouds of dust blew across the tracks and became pools of black mud and water, for it was raining just about as hard as it could. Between each pair of rails was a long shallow canal on which the flickering light from the gas-lamps cast wavering circles while the lights themselves shone out dimly trying to penetrate the gloom of black dust and heavy rain.

I was returning from a message to the nearby dock stores and had on oilskins and rubber boots. I stopped near a lamp to await the passing of a shunted car coming along on which line I could not judge owing to the darkness. It passed and I was about to continue my floundering way, when something pressed against my leg. I gave a jump, looked down, saw nothing, but still felt distinctly a moving pressure of some living thing. Then a gust of wind cleared the lights for a second and I saw a soaking wet tabby cat, jet black like the night itself, leaning and rubbing against me. As I bent to it, it gave a pitiful meaow.

"Now, kitty," I protested, "what I am to do with you, I don't know. But I can't leave you here to be run over or drowned." She meaowed again and I picked her up and took her with me. Even the warmth of my body through the wet oilskin seemed to make her feel better and before I had reached the ship, I could feel the vibrations of a purr. I made up my mind that this would not be the ship's cat, but the Mate's.

Aboard, I went to my room and dragged some pieces of canvas out of a locker to make her a bed. I went to the pantry and got some condensed milk, which I took back to my room again where she awaited me, now purring like a four horse-power dynamo. After a big drink of milk, she fell asleep and I did the same.

In the morning, I tried to impress her with the fact that she was to be my cat. I brushed her with a shoe brush. Beneath the grime she remained as black as coal except for a V-shaped patch of white on her neck, like a white shirt front. When she was moderately clean, I set her down and took a look at her. She was the oddest looking cat you ever saw. She had such short legs that the fur on her tummy touched the floor. "Have you a name?" I asked her, but she didn't even purr. "Well," I declared, "I've a good one for you—Short Legs—and you're my cat, understand? The ship has one already and no monkey tricks with her, mind you. She's as uppity as you make them. Stick to your own end of the ship and you'll be alright."

She blinked at me a couple of times and rubbed against my leg again which suited me pretty well for an answer.

My door opened directly onto the main deck, hence the door-step was formed by the coamings or foundation of the house. It was about 15 inches high which kept out the water in moderate weather. In stormy weather, when there was a lot of water on the deck, the door had to be tightly closed. The cracks of the lower half door were filled with oakum or caulked, for often the water became three or four feet deep outside, sometimes even reaching to the top of it.

Short Legs had many things to learn about ships. The very first day at sea, after leaving Cardiff, she was sitting on the doorstep when I came down off watch at Eight Bells (noon). There was quite a sea running and two or three inches of water streaming from the side of the main deck as the ship rolled. Short Legs was watching it with popping eyes, all astonishment, as if to say, "What kind of a backyard is this, if you please?" Then, seeing me, she jumped down to greet me and was promptly swept off her feet by the water. She gave one awful "yowl" as she shot across the deck toward the lee scuppers at about a mile a minute.

I dashed after her, fearing she might go right out one of the scupper holes and overboard. She made a wild spring for my legs instead and it was my turn to yell for her claws were sharp and she was taking no chances. I reached down, grabbed her by the scruff of the neck, tossed her into the room and shut the door.

I didn't see my cat in the dog-watch when I came down to tea, but at midnight when I came below, I found her coiled on the old canvas, moaning. I thought perhaps she had licked too much salt water from her wet fur and was sick from it, but I soon saw that she was suffering from honest-to-goodness seasickness. I had brought her some milk and a bit of meat but she moaned more than before when I showed food to her.

"Well, well, Short Legs," I told her, "you are no seaman's cat, as I might have known before. But there are only two things to be done about seasickness—get used to it, or get over it. I'm afraid I can't do anything to help you. Goodnight." And I turned in.

In the morning, she was feeling fine and I accepted her as a pretty good sailor, after all.

Many days after this, the ship was in the north-east Trade

Winds, sailing down past the Cape de Verde Islands and not far off the African coast. It is a place where hot winds from the Sahara desert often sweep numbers of swallows out to sea, causing them to alight on passing vessels. This voyage was no exception and many alighted on the *Erin's Isle*, some flying through the open portholes right into the rooms. Two came into my quarters and perched in the rim of the porthole. Short Legs spied them and her hunting instinct was immediately aroused. She dashed round and round the room trying to discover some way of getting near the porthole. Suddenly it dawned on her that she could do so by means of the bed curtain and she was up it like an Able Seaman or a lineman up a telephone pole. She balanced herself on the curtain rod, then she climbed onto the pole with the hope of getting footing for a spring. But the rod deceived her, and she did a cartwheel around the slippery brass and flopped into the bunk while the swallows flew away.

Short Legs was disgusted. She coiled up on the bunk and went to sleep. Ah, but it was a cat-nap alright, asleep with one eye open!

The poor swallows were terribly thirsty and came back again, looking for fresh water. There was water in the basin on the stand by the wall and they must have seen it on their first visit. There was a great deal of twittering as they discussed the advisability of flying right into the room. Finally one seemed to say to the other, "Wait. I'll show you," and it fluttered across and landed on the edge of the basin. It bent to take a drink and as it did so, the one on the porthole rim began twittering to beat the band. But the thirsty bird was too busy to notice the warning sound. Short Legs had come to life with a snap and a leap. She came down right on top of the swallow. She skidded into the basin, but held her catch in a death grip while she did so.

I had been sitting on the hatch watching the drama through the doorway and although I dashed in at once and grabbed

Short Legs, making her drop the bird, it was too late. The swallow was dead. I gave Short Legs a couple of spanks and tossed her away from me. I was angry with her yet realized that she was only acting upon instinct. But the other swallow, poor thing, miles and miles from home was flying round and round the deck in the vicinity of the porthole, twittering wildly for its mate. I watched it sadly, but I was wasting my sympathies, for a hawk, which had also taken refuge on the ship, spied it at once. It drove the swallow lower and lower until, flying frantically over the sea, it fell into the water. The pursuer wheeled to pick it up, but as the hawk stretched out its talons to grab the still fluttering swallow, the crest of a small wave reached for the hawk and in a second of time, while they struggled vainly, both disappeared astern.

After watching this strange tragedy, I went back into my room, the bird which I had taken from the cat still in my hand. The unashamed animal came leaping from the distant corner of the room and I dropped the bird to her. She sniffed it, touched it with her paw, and walked away. I had left the door open. She went out onto the deck and for the rest of that day would have nothing to do with me.

During my years of seafaring, I had many experiences with animals and birds which I chose to take with me, sometimes for pleasure only, sometimes that I might study the habits of their species.

I took a land tortoise with me on one occasion when trading in the West Indies. It was an odd-looking thing. When it hauled in its head and tail you couldn't tell which end went first, and the ends of its toes stuck out under its shell like wheels below a fender on an automobile.

I have seen many kinds of turtles on my journeys but the most famous one was a real ocean turtle which sailed around the world with me in a tub.

This turtle was one of the Hawksbill variety. Although not a tortoise it supplied us with real tortoise shell.

Our ship was becalmed in the ocean southwest of the Azores and in a northeast extension of the Sargasso Sea. It was the 28th day of August and the latitude forty north and forty-two west. I was standing at the rail looking around for signs of life or possible wreckage among the weedy islands. I could scarcely believe my eyes when I spied this species of turtle since it is rarely found so far north. I decided at once to catch this fellow if possible.

I ordered a boat launched and with four apprentices we rowed toward the spot where I had seen the Hawksbill. As we came near, we turned the boat gently round with the stern toward the turtle. I sat ready to grab him as the boys backed us nearer. He was smaller than I thought and I was afraid that he might wake and be out of sight before my hands could reach him.

"We'll use the scoop net," I whispered, for a human voice might startle him.

I sank the net cautiously under the weeds, then lifted it quickly. He made frantic efforts to escape, but one of the apprentices scrambled alongside of me in the stern and held the net while I grabbed for the turtle, and got him!

When I released him, he raced fore and aft, the length of the boat, in wild excitement; then as he became exhausted, I picked him up by the two edges of his shell to have a better look at him. He worked his flippers and his neck frantically to get hold of my hands, but tired himself out doing it and became calmer.

He was quite tiny and certainly not very old; yet I knew he must be at least a year old to be there at all, for the eggs from which these turtles are hatched, when laid, are buried in the sands of the Keys off Florida or Nassau, some 2,100 miles away. They drift from there with the Sargasso weed along the margin of the Gulf Stream and the great northeast drift of the Atlantic, and require at least a year to reach the spot in which I found him.

It didn't take us long to row back to the ship. As soon as

we arrived there, I had a tub filled with sea-water and dumped the turtle into it. He was pleased to be in water again but mystified by the close quarters assigned to him. He kept swimming slowly round and round the tub, hour after hour, resembling the action of an animal in the zoo that paces back and forth, back and forth, never resting for a moment. Although I put some pieces of fresh fish into the water, he would eat nothing and it was several days before he became interested in investigating the food offered him, then he took a nibble or two of canned meat. Salted meat he would not touch.

I was afraid we were going to lose him, those first few days, for his appetite was so poor; but he lived on. We soon got into cooler weather and another difficulty arose. The water in the tub was changed every day. Every day it was just a little cooler than the day before, and, although it was still early in September, as the ship travelled toward her destination, which was Limerick, Ireland, through the waters of the famous Shannon River, the water was much colder than that to which the turtle was accustomed. He stopped eating altogether again. Then we conceived the idea of heating several kettles of sea-water and adding it to his "bath" which he liked so well that when it cooled off, he would begin scratching and scratching at the side of the tub with his flippers to inform us that it was time to add more. I don't know what he lived on for he still refused food, even the nice fresh fish which we bought for him from the fishermen at Limerick.

From Limerick, we went on to Port Talbot in South Wales to load coal for Chile. While in port, we used some of the water there to heat our turtle and when it was poured into the tub, he went round and round it as if a couple of killer whales or a shark were chasing him. I said to myself, "I've made his bath too hot," and put my hand down to feel. The temperature was as he usually liked it. Then I remembered someone telling me that fresh water is poison to certain forms of ocean life. So that was the trouble! But it was not so easy to remedy it;

for we couldn't get ocean water unless we went outside of the dock gates and dipped it from the Bristol Channel and that certainly could not be done. Suddenly it occurred to me to try using ordinary salt in the fresh water. This I did and the turtle calmed down and seemed satisfied. But he ate nothing until we filled his tub from the ocean again.

We called him Tutankhamen because there was a great deal in the papers at that time about King Tut of Egypt. For short we called him Tut.

As soon as our ship sailed away from British shores and into warmer regions, Tut woke up and developed an enormous appetite. Up to the time of this voyage, we had only an ordinary tub for our pet, and when in port, while most of us lived on shore, we had given him the bathtub. Now we made him a square one, like a deep box, which held quite a lot of water. It had a slanty shelf at one end on which he could crawl and take a sun bath if he wanted to get out for a while.

As the ship went south, toward the tropics, an odd flying fish came on board. One day I found one in the tub with Tut who was trying to swallow it whole and making a pretty mess of it. Probably he had never seen such a fish before. Anyway, he had gotten its head into his mouth and was choking and frantically dragging at it with his two front flippers. I rushed for a spoon and pried his jaws apart with the handle, then slowly dragged out the fish. He had it about half swallowed and the head, which is around 7 inches long, must have been nearly to his stomach. The experience affected him as a human being is affected by getting a fish bone into his throat. He wouldn't look at that particular kind of food for weeks after, but lived on pieces of canned meat.

Tut had grown fast in spite of the cold and the finicky appetite. I was very proud of him.

Soon we crossed the Equator and went down through the southern tropics to the mouth of the great Rio de la Plata. There are very violent storms in this region, known as pamperos.

One of the forerunners of such storms is vast clouds of moths, butterflies, and dragon flies, blown from the land ahead of the storm or flying away from it. One of these storms occurred while we were there, bringing a rain of moths before it which covered the ship and entered the rooms as well, even making a blanket on the water of Tut's tub. To my astonishment, Tut was pleased and accepted them as a kind of delicacy which he ate and ate until I thought he would burst. But almost as he finished his feast, he felt a shiver go up and down his spine. It was the pampero itself, bringing a sudden change in temperature. Before long, he drew his head and flippers into his shell as far as he could and lay motionless. Then, once more, we had to remove him to the bathtub where we could keep him warmer, adding heated water to his bath as we had done before.

In this way, he weathered the miseries of Cape Horn. Sometimes the storms there were so violent and the motion of the ship so pronounced that we could scarcely keep water in the tub and poor old Tut was washed back and forth, hour after hour. I guess he must have lost a lot of sleep. As soon as we were around the Cape, we brought him up onto the deck to his own tub once more. The warm air and the calmer sea were more comfortable for him.

There were times when we were all so busy on board that Tut was forgotten. But we learned that he could go without food for as long as a month so we did not worry greatly.

He certainly had rather a remarkable experience for a turtle. One of his greatest passages was from Vancouver all the way down to Cape Horn, then across the South Atlantic up to Africa and to the port of East London. During the warm part of this trip, he again tried the flying fish, with success this time, for his jaws had grown much stronger and he could now cut clean bites out of the fish, leaving the bones for someone else to deal with. And that "someone" was a cat that had come on board the ship at Vancouver. But this cat thought that Tut himself must be good to eat also, and in fine weather would sit for hours on the corner of his tub watching him swim around and trying to hook him with her paw when he came up for breath. All turtles come up to breathe, having lungs and not gills. Tut would let out his breath, making a noise like "pouf," and sort of wink at the cat, then sink down again to safety.

At East London it was holiday time, being near Christmas and summer in that part of the world, and many visitors came on board ship to have a look around. They were entirely too interested in Tut for his comfort. Some of them were very inquisitive and much worse than the cat in the way they express-ed their curiosity. They would lift the poor turtle out of his tub and lay him on his back on the deck, poking him in the tummy with their umbrellas and canes to make him wave his flippers for their entertainment. This would not do. We put a stop to it by fitting wires across the top of the tub. The cat liked the wire netting immensely as she could sit or lie on it comfortably all day, watching Tut and giving him little dabs with her paw when he came up. Tut did not mind this in the least. He seemed to feel much safer and was therefore happier with the protection above him. Finally the cat tired of such quiet amusement and left him pretty much alone.

From East London, the ship went on to Port Pirie in South Australia and then, once more, around Cape Horn to Silloth in the North of England and on from there to Cardiff, Wales. Here Tut made a journey by train, his first and his last, to another ship, the *Elginshire*, which I was to command. He was carried to Barry in an ordinary grip though he had grown quite a lot, and his tub was sent by freight. He travelled from there to Santos, Brazil, and then to north-west Australia where we stayed for three months. We then returned to Liverpool.

The Great War was on now, and no one could live on ships in the docks, so when the cold weather came, it was quite certain that poor old Tut would die. I saw nothing for it but to kill him, rather than have him suffer a lingering death. I did this with great regret. We might consider him a war victim as were many millions of humans. I had kept him for four years and two months, and his travellings covered 122,964 nautical miles, once completely around the world. Although he did not live so very long, he had an unusual experience for a turtle.

Turtles grow very slowly and, in spite of his occasional periods of fasting, he had grown remarkably. When I caught him, he was just 8 inches long, and when killed, he measured 18 inches.

I am often asked why I didn't make turtle soup of him.

He was not the kind of turtle that is usually used for soup, and in the second place, he was like a pet to me. I wouldn't have relished him. In fact, I do not care for any food made from this animal. It is very strong smelling and if its fat gets in with the meat when frying, or in the soup, the strongest stomach does not hold it easily. One good whiff of cooking turtle was enough for me any time.

Although I did not like to interfere with the natural life of any creature on land or sea, I felt justified in keeping Tut aboard to study his species. We did our best to make him happy. When we were lying becalmed in parts of the ocean similar in condition to his home waters, we sometimes gave him a swim.

We first considered tying a string to one of his flippers and letting him down this way. But we were afraid of interfering with his circulation and perhaps losing him. Instead, I decided to bore a hole in the edge of his shell. The shell had no feeling in it. The flesh and connecting skin around flippers and tail do not extend to within a quarter inch of the shell's edge. It was like putting a hole through a finger nail beyond where it joins the flesh of the finger.

I chose a spot right over my turtle's tail and only one-eighth inch in diameter. In this way the weight of the line was at the back and did not pull him sideways.

I'll never forget the first time I let Tut down into the sea. He was off like a speed boat, until he came to the end of the string, and then he cut up such a fuss that I had to bring him back to the ship and lift him out. I had thought he would swim about in different directions, as a dog runs about when fastened to a long chain, but this was not his way. He seemed happy to be back in the tub and swam slowly around and around it as if really relishing its safety. But after a few trials in the sea, he learned to enjoy his supervised freedom too.

It is surprising what confidence even a captured turtle develops under consistently kind treatment. I regretted bringing his fairly pleasant life to an end, but if he had remained in the Sargasso, who knows, his life might have been shorter.

# A Voyage on the Arctic Stream

Before I signed on the *Erin's Isle* as Boy I had travelled by sail 141,000 land miles. While a member of her crew, advancing finally to A.B., I sailed another 318,256 land miles. These were important years of learning and of many unforgettable adventures.

The *Erin's Isle*, though undergoing the roughest treatment, was seaworthy for more than half a century. Wooden ships of her time, if constructed of oak or teak and built by careful workmen, sometimes lasted as long as sixty or seventy years. Indeed the hardwoods which I have mentioned were almost indestructible and windjammers were made ready to withstand severe rigours of time and tide.

I am glad that my seafaring career began and ended in a windjammer. Because of my early experiences as a skipper's son who sailed with him on many exciting voyages, the term of training as a crew member before I became Captain of the *Arctic Stream* was considerably less than that of other ambitious A.B.'s.

The *Arctic Stream* was a full-rigged ship. We set out from Glasgow for Portland, Oregon. We suffered a week from contrary winds before we got out of the Straits of Dover. Once away from the Straits we passed quickly enough through the north-east Trades and entered that area of calm between West Africa and Brazil known as "the doldrums."

I had a difficult crew, a mixture of nationalities, but with careful handling they worked together faithfully and I was proud of them by the time we reached Oregon.

The north-east and south-east Trades are fairly close together along the Brazilian coast but very far apart towards Africa. We wanted to get into the south-east Trades as soon as possible but there was a strong contrary current off Brazil to be avoided. We were becalmed for two weeks between Trades.

During this time we did a lot of fishing. In the clear green water, sea life was visible for more than 100 feet down: sharks, big and small, as well as fish of many other kinds, including flying fish.

In my mind, Trade Winds, flying fish and fine weather are closely associated.

A story told among seamen illustrates the fact that truth is stranger than fiction. A sailor boy returning from his first foreign voyage, in telling his mother of wonders he had seen, referred to "mountains of sugar that didn't melt, floating in rivers of rum, and fish with wings that flew over the ship and even came on board." His mother advised him to stick to the truth. Mountains of sugar there might be, and rivers of rum, but flying fish – that was too much for his poor old mother to believe.

To sailors, all Trade Wind and tropical weather is known as "flying fish weather." Sometimes seamen who regularly sailed in ships going down across the Equator were scornfully called "flying fish sailors" by those who voyaged across the stormy Atlantic.

A flying fish does wonderful things but it does not fly in the true meaning of the word. It is, however, a past master in gliding, performing many tricks unknown to gliders on land such as the flying squirrel.

The transparent and glistening wings of this fish look very much as if in rapid motion. But the fish cannot use these expanded fins as a bird does its wings. It cannot flap them. It cannot increase its speed in the air with them, but must wait until it sinks almost to the surface of the sea. When the lower lobe of the tail touches the water, by means of a few sharp thrusts, the fish is in the air again. But while in the air, it cannot increase its speed. It resembles a small outboard motor boat with a propeller extending below the keel; if the boat were raised slightly off the surface of the water, the propeller would still touch and drive it along.

The fish cannot change the direction of flight while in the air, only by a flick of its tail when the tail touches the water. However, if flying across the wind the direction of its flight may be slowly altered as it loses velocity curving away from the wind's force. If it takes off in sudden fright against a stiff gale, it is often thrown high in the air out of control and may land on a ship's deck. If flying at night, it seems to reach a higher altitude and is attracted by light. This brings it to lighted ships, or so we believe. I have no proof of this but certainly fishers of fliers use lights to attract them, and the fish come on deck more often by night than by day.

They are sometimes called "the lazy man's fish." The manner of fishing was to take out a small sail boat after dark with a lantern hung in the centre of the sail on the windward side, then to sail back and forward with the wind on the side or beam. The fish would fly at the light, hit the sail, and fall down into the boat.

A large sailing ship with sides quite high out of the water seldom received one of these fish as a visitor. The *Arctic Stream* entertained only two although we saw many thousands. As an experiment, for three nights we draped a tarpaulin like a huge square curtain over the ship's side and with two cords attached to the lower corners, raised the corners a little, forming a pocket close to the water. We hung a light in the centre of the tarpaulin but never a fish did we catch. However, the Second Mate who slept on the weather side with his port hole open, was reading in his bunk one warm night, when a fish came through the port hole, hit the bunk side like a bullet and fell wildly flapping on the man's chest. He gave a yell of terror although the poor thing didn't hurt him, and he had his revenge by having it cooked in oil for breakfast the next morning.

The flying fish is commonly about 8 or 9 inches in length like a trout or large smelt, and the Second Mate declared the flavour was delicious.

Once in the South Atlantic during a fierce gale one came aboard that measured 16 inches. It was thrown up by the wind so high that it hit one of the masts and fell to the deck. Also, I have seen very tiny ones, barely visible from the ship, about the size of your fingernail, wings and all.

Small flying fish are numerous in the Sargasso Sea. One species there is the colour of the weeds with fringed wings, and another with four wings like a dragon fly. On some, the wings are like silver cellophane, on others dark red.

There is one called the Flying Gunard. This is not a true flying fish. It is found near tropical Australia and, I think, near the Indies. The Gunard has large wings of most gorgeous blue and gold and crimson and purple in various patterns. Gunards do not use their wings to fly but as ornaments to open and shut like a beautiful fan.

The true flying fish has a rough time of it for it is preyed upon by the larger fishes. The dolphin catches it in mid-air but prefers to follow its shadow and to meet it at the end of its flight as it touches the water's surface.

Second in interest to us as we lay becalmed were the numerous sharks. We were careful when we ventured out from the ship in a small boat to carry equipment with us to meet an attack if it came – a pistol, a shark hook baited with salt pork, and several harpoons. But although the sharks swam fairly close at times, we were not troubled by them. However, we did not venture out except in bright daylight. But the Mate tried to hook one from the deck of the ship. This shark had been circling us for several hours and although we were safe enough on board, nobody liked the look of him.

The shark hook was baited with a small piece of salt pork

and lowered over the rail to the water's surface. Almost as soon as the hook touched the water the shark glided over to it, and as the lead line was slackened by the Mate and trailed slowly, the hook vanished under the shark. We held our breath, only to see him turn away and disappear astern.

"He's not too old but he's wise," the Mate muttered, adding hopefully, "But he had a smell of that pork and he liked it."

He was not a big fellow, about 10 feet long. His birthplace had been the open sea. He may have belonged to the deep sea fauna, capable of existing a thousand fathoms below the ocean's surface. I was not sure of his species (there are at least 150), but of his nature there was no doubt: he was equipped with rows of large triangular teeth, deeply notched. His grin was frightening. He was a man-eating shark, perhaps hoping that someone would fall overboard. We had a rather timid lad as Boy on that trip and I noticed him move away from the rail.

The shark was coming back. He swam confidently and quite fast. As he would have taken the meat, the Mate let the lead line loose and then brought it tight with a jerk. There was fierce threshing about in the water. The shark was hooked. The Second Mate shouted for help and several of the watch came running. They took hold of the line with him. The shark was too large to be landed on the poop deck. They dragged it along and brought it up on the main deck. Still threshing about wildly it knocked down two of the crew before another slipped a piece of wood under its tail and brought down the axe. In a few seconds the creature lay still, his life blood streaming from him.

We kept the backbone for a walking stick and the fins, which are a delicacy, were cooked for supper. The body was cut up and thrown into the sea, and also a sucker which we found under and attached to the shark. The head of a sucker is corrugated and it was difficult to pry loose.

After the deck was washed up, we all had a careful look into the sea. Would other sharks come to investigate the unnatural state of the water which was coloured red in patches where we had tossed pieces of the carcass? But none came. Two days later, the wind came up and we were away.

As I mentioned before, it was never my object to kill for the sake of killing. We killed at sea for safety, for food, or for the purpose of study.

We kept the head of the shark long enough to examine its structure, especially the mouth and teeth. There was a full row of teeth with several other rows behind it, nicely packed as it were, to be erected at the smell of food or upon attack.

Sharks' teeth seem to be mounted like those of a modern saw, with a jawbone thin enough to follow the teeth into any cut they might make to almost any depth. The teeth are not rigid like ours. When biting on a hard substance, they tip over as on a hinge. Behind the main row I counted five other rows. I have heard that a certain species adds a row of teeth for every year of life, but I don't believe this.

During my years at sea, according to my log book, we caught and I examined at least one hundred sharks. Practically every one had an empty stomach and never at any time did I find anything to suggest that the shark had attacked a human being.

I would sooner encounter a shark than a large crab. The latter can move so fast one can hardly see it. In one bite it can nip out a hunk of flesh big enough to mortally wound.

Sharks as long as 40 feet have been found in tropical waters. These are most dangerous man-eating sharks. A female has been known to give birth to 30 infant sharks at a time.

In India and China a substance from shark fins is made into gelatin and is an important article of trade.

During our voyages, we came upon so many interesting types of sea life that it would take a whole book to describe them.

# Further Adventures
# on the Arctic Stream

If the waters off Cape Horn had given up their dead in the days of sailing ships, perhaps fewer men would have "signed on" if required to round the Cape. Many a shipwreck or lesser disaster resulting in the untimely end of lives went uncharted or unexplained in the annals of nautical history. "Whereabouts unknown", "Mysteriously disappeared", "Presumed lost", might refer to the vessel or one or more of its crew. Men of the sea knew this and expected no other epitaph. Often with outward calm, they refused to desert a captain who may have been more concerned with preserving his ship and his honour than with saving his life and the lives of his crew.

On my second trip in command around the Horn, the weather was especially ugly. Again my crew was made up of many nationalities, some experienced, some new to sea life.

As we worked our way down the South Atlantic, meeting blow after blow, all hands were often on duty, and, reasonably enough, men in need of sleep, overworked and anxious, were quarrelsome. Often I heard loud angry voices in the fo'c'sle, and twice the Mate called on me to interfere in personal quarrels between a hot-headed Irish cook and his helper, a West Indian. On one occasion the cook lost a tooth and the helper received an ugly blow on the head. Sometimes I wondered while we lay waiting for favourable winds or fought to control our ship through days and nights of storm as we drew nearer to the

Cape, as grumbling and angry looks increased: "Are we in danger of more serious trouble than the struggle against wind and wave? Are these the symptoms of a Captain's greatest fear—a mutiny?"

But before we reached the Cape, a common danger preceded by a strange phenomenon united us, and personal differences were forgotten.

Just off Rio de la Plata the sea began to make waves that were of an alarming height—35 to 40 feet. The sky darkened. We were encountering a Pampero, a fierce storm common to that area.

The shore was 300 miles away but a strange experience was the coming upon us of flying land insects, many highly coloured butterflies and hundreds of little birds. The wind had blown them out to sea, and we were their first point of resting. The poor creatures in thousands covered our ship and clung wherever there was a place to cling to or lit upon rigging, sails, railings, even the shoulders of the man at the wheel. Those of us merciful enough brushed them aside on the deck floor to avoid crushing them.

The clouds blackened and I called all hands. They were scarcely ready when the storm struck forcing the ship to heel so far over that her rail was submerged.

By five o'clock that afternoon the blackness had settled over us as if it were midnight. The Mate's voice could scarcely be heard for the shrieking of the wind and the creaking and groaning of the *Arctic Stream* as she plunged forward almost engulfed, and with the spray blinding the helmsman as he tried to hold her steady. The Second Mate went to his assistance. The raging waters seemed determined to gain control.

I was proud of the conduct of my crew. The Second Mate, Robinson, had been at sea twenty years. He was known to be a grumbler but that night with set lips he directed wherever he was needed, without complaint. He would be a ship's master some day, I thought, and a good one!

In the darkness it was impossible to be merciful to the creatures who had sought shelter with us. Sea boots made a crunching sound as the crew worked feverishly. We knew what was happening but we had the good ship and ourselves to save.

As the sea struck over the weather-rail, I saw a strange thing happen. A young Swede, who had been relieved of his work at one of the hand pumps by our Cockney carpenter for a minute, drew a letter from his pocket. In the light of the binnacle–the only light visible, faintly glimmering through the heavy spume–he bent over it. A minute–a few words–it could not have been more and then the letter was held to his lips before being returned to his pocket.

Love before death in a storm, I thought, as a horrible shudder passed through the ship. The Swede had a special reason for living. He would stay at his post. He took over a pump and no one ever worked a hand pump harder. More than muscle makes a man strong.

The sea charged down roller after roller until I ordered the fire lit under the boiler and the winch attached and connected to the pumps, for we could not keep ourselves from being flooded, by hand. "There is three feet of water in the hold," one reported, and I heard a deck boy on his first voyage crying into his sleeve.

"Are we going down, sir?" a former landlubber from London ventured as I stopped to watch him trying to help carry out the Mate's order to lower away the topsails. We had already taken in all but six and the foresail.

How could I answer him honestly? "Work like the devil, man," I roared, "and stop shivering. She's never gone down–she never will."

Under my breath I added, "Please God." And at that moment there was a vivid flash like a gilded knife opening the bowels of the heavens. Deafening thunder followed and through the blackness such torrents of rain that it all but choked us as it fell.

The scuppers couldn't carry it off fast enough. We worked

ankle-deep in it and with every opening of the house door, it forced its way in.

A man tended the fire under the boiler in the donkey-room all that night while the ship's carpenter looked to the winch and fittings so that we heard the reassuring sound of the pumps that told us that the water below was still deep enough for alarm.

The wind screamed with the voice of a hurricane. We had survived many a storm but this time–the *Arctic Stream* trembled as if shaken by an earthquake with no surcease. Would we founder? Even the planking beneath our feet vibrated. We sank deeper and deeper in the raging sea. Now nothing on deck was visible. We saw only the attacking white spume. The flicker of light on the poop became the only sign of life.

Under the levelling force of the rain the tall waves lost their frightening height. Slowly the pumps slackened their efforts. After a night of fighting for her life, of plunging, rolling, angling under the press of water and wind until the lee rail and a portion of the deck were travelling below water, the *Arctic Stream* righted herself. With dawn the storm clouds scurried off–what was left of them after the rain–and the sun came smiling over the horizon.

We threw off our dripping oilskins. We were wet through but the wind had died down and the cook was busy in the galley. The men stood together with plates of hot stew and mugs of nourishing cocoa. I stood among them. They were happy with a sense of victory. A motley crew? Inexperienced for the most part, but I was proud of the way they had met their first challenge–and a critical one. I told them so.

Even as I spoke I saw the Swede fumbling in his pocket for the letter which was surely soaking wet and probably unreadable. But the heart of man remembers.

# A Fateful Shipwreck

What are a man's thoughts during perilous storms at sea? I believe that very few sailors think of death until the crucial moment has all but come. They must listen for the voice of Captain or Mate shouting orders through what is usually a howling blast accompanied by lashing water and the creaking of timbers. From Boy to A.B., all unite in an effort to ease the burden of the straining vessel. They are under fire as certainly as soldiers on land attacked by the enemy. And as soldiers in battle they must trust their officers in command.

But, however trusting, however brave and loyal to duty, the threat of unleashed natural forces is beyond the imagination of those who have not experienced them. With stormy heavens above and enveloping seas below, the sailor has no haven of safety but his ship. He thinks of himself as part of her and so grows a love which only seamen understand.

Only one man in that storm off the Cape had voiced fear and this he had couched in the form of a question.

While the carpenter disconnected the emergency pump equipment and the rest of the men off watch helped to tidy the dishevelled ship, I took a look to east and west, wondering how other ships had fared. There was the Yankee clipper which had passed us in full sail the afternoon before the storm struck. Our Cockney had muttered disgust that we cautiously travelled in half sail but I had an eye on the barometer and a nose to the wind.

I looked for the Cockney now. Yes, he was watching as the clipper limped past us toward port somewhere, her sails in shreds and her main mast splintered. I hoped that when taken by surprise she had lost no one overboard.

As I went to my cabin for a needed rest, I saw a gleam of bright blue and gold, about the size of a sixpence inserted in a crevice by the cabin door. It was a tattered-of-wing butterfly. I had almost forgotten the rain of little creatures blown to shelter upon us before the pre-storm winds. I rescued the poor thing and carried it on the palm of my hand into the cabin. I laid it gently on the cloth cover of my chest. It was alive but after an attempt or two to use its soaked and torn wings it lay forever still. Sadly I carried it out and dropped it into the sea which had swept away its companions. But to my surprise a day later I found a small bird, much like a field sparrow, living but with a broken leg, in a coil of rope near the poop. I made a splint from a match stick and gave the poor thing the freedom of my cabin, feeding and watering it several times a day, but its condition was so frail that it did not survive.

The sea began to make again and we encountered several blows before we were safely around the Cape. But before we left the South Atlantic we were confronted by an awesome sight In what may be called Antarctic Regions, I think, we saw a great white object more than a mile long, L-shaped, flat-topped, and ghostly in appearance. The night was clear with a distinct chill in the wind and a half moon. Shafts of moonlight danced like sprites along the upper area of the object.

I shouted for all hands. We were within a mile of an iceberg, the largest I was ever to see. It resembled a floating marble mountain, with a chiselled top.

Thank God, I thought, it does not stand in our course. A part of it was submerged, lying in wait, it seemed to us, for unwary seamen. To southward a dark thing could be seen bobbing up and down like a top.

"A piece of wood, maybe," I said grimly, "all that is left of somebody's good ship. And there would be no survivors in a case like that. Remember the Titanic? No ship is unsinkable. This berg has probably floated down from the North Atlantic. I'm glad we didn't catch up with her."

Our course lay at least five miles south-west of her and we were in control. The stormy waters would be calm by morning we believed.

My sleep was disturbed several times, first by the arrival of the Mate at midnight and again at 2 a.m.

"I think, sir, the berg's floating this way," he said. "Should we furl and drop anchor until we're certain?"

"No," I said. "We may have to go off course. But I'll take a look at her."

This I did through the binoculars. True, she looked menacing and larger but it was the effect of the moonlight—an illusion. If moving our way, it was moving so slowly that we would be safely out of its reach in plenty of time. But I was uneasy. At 4 a.m, I went up on deck. It was darker now. The moon and the scattering of stars were hidden by a curtain of cloud. Might there be an unsuspected projection below sea level as well as the part we knew to be submerged?

We had one close call. We did not want another. The man at the wheel was the young Swede, a capable helmsman. He welcomed me.

"She's a brute that thing out there, sir," he said, "but with a fair wind we'll soon leave her behind. I never saw one close and I hope I won't again."

There was quite a sea running now, but he was handling the wheel wonderfully well. I told him so.

"There's no need for alarm," I reassured. "As you say, we'll be away in plenty of time."

But I did not retire to my cabin again until nightfall. It was to be a strange blood-curdling day for our crew.

After the sun tipped the East I noted again the bobbing dark spot, now closer to us by perhaps half a mile.

I stood looking into the sun as it rose. Then it was hidden behind the berg and the sea separating us darkened into a shadowy green. The bobbing object changed in outline. A shaft went up with a flutter of white on the top. Only for half a minute, then it toppled, seeming to fall behind whatever the object was.

Chips, the carpenter, had been mending a spar near the stern. He came running. "Sir—oh, sir," he said, "There's a poor bloke on that spot of wreck out there. I seen him signal. I seen it with my bare eyes, sir. Top of an oar—his shirt maybe—white like. Sir, we gotta do something."

Of course we had to do something. "You're right," I said. "Lower the gig. I'll go and I need four men to row, and I want volunteers. There's a serious risk. I want only sailors ready to take it."

No true seaman ever left another to the mercy of the sea. The greater the peril the greater the need for chivalry.

I did not lack for volunteers and the young Swede was one of them.

The sea was rough but not rough for that region. We were soon on our way. I was somewhat skeptical as to the wisdom and necessity of what we were doing, however, because from the time we left the *Arctic Stream* none of us could detect any sign of life on what again became but a floating piece of wreckage.

But after half a mile it was possible to define a shape—that of a small raft or boat.

We found that the distance to be covered was closer to two miles than to one.

"If there's a man in that boat, he's a dead one," said Gillis, a Scot. "There hasn't been any signalling and I've had the glass more up than down—no movement either. There's a kind of hump but that could be anything."

The Swede put all his strength into the business of rowing. As I said before, he had a reason to live, that boy, and he wanted others to live too. His face was a study in anxiety and determination. He was a lad I would have liked for a son.

"There's a man in that thing," he said, "and he's alive."

Both the Scot and the Swede were right. It wasn't a boat but a raft of the kind sometimes carried by French ships. It was afternoon before we came close enough to see the occupants. When about half a mile away we saw something to curdle our blood – the water around the raft and toward us was infested by sharks. In a company they encircled the floating raft, tossing and churning the water and darting under and up again.

Our boys were waiting, I knew, for the word from me to turn back, but I said, "Don't let them scare you, fellows, but get the harpoons ready just in case. They aren't after us – aren't interested in us. They're just annoyed by our arrival. They have an appetite for the dead. They're getting impatient, too. Look at them."

They were hungry. They struck the raft with their powerful dorsal fins underneath and it flopped this way and that, lifting out of the water; but each time it fell back right side up.

Meanwhile, a figure bent over with arms folded and head on chest, probably lifeless, flopped with it, but remained in the raft somehow, as if his legs were tied there. He was hatless and the upper part of his body was naked and blistered by exposure. Later we learned that he had been in that position for many days.

As we moved closer, Davy, an apprentice, threw a harpoon and there was wild excitement among the sharks. Davy had aimed well but although the water was red with blood, the shark, aided by his kind, made a get-away. But it was a successful throw for the attackers swam off long enough for us to row up to the raft.

"Lose no time," I shouted. We pulled alongside and manoeuvring with our oars, we tipped the raft toward us while the unconscious figure was drawn into the boat.

The raft, we quickly saw, could not be boarded. It was on the verge of sinking from leakage through a hole the sharks had torn with their teeth on the bottom.

146

The man, though unconscious, was alive. But it was not the living in which the sharks were interested. Lying flat was a partly decomposed body. "We'll dump the raft over and let them have him while we get away," I ordered, and this was done.

The stench in the air was horrible as we rowed back to the ship. It clung to the half-dead victim we had taken, who must have lived in close proximity to his dead companion for many days, perhaps weeks.

We hailed a Dutch freighter with a doctor on board a few hours later. The senseless, half-starved Frenchman was transferred to the Dutch steamer. The doctor explained that his body had not been nourished by food or water for so long that there was no hope of his recovery. He had probably shared with his companion what little, if any, they had salvaged.

His feet were bare and swollen to twice their normal size, as were his tongue and lips. He wore one article of clothing— seaman's trousers. There were no identifying marks and no articles to tell us who he was or in what ship he had sailed. Perhaps he and his friend had tried to make a get-away from an intolerable master. Perhaps a noble craft had come into contact with the giant berg and lay at the bottom of the sea. But no French ship was reported missing in that region at the time.

There was nothing to be done but to sail on into kinder waters, thankful for our own safety.

The Swede, fingering his now unreadable letter, continued to brood over the fate of the two Frenchmen. They had been young men and somewhere, no doubt, love had been waiting for their return.

# The Travelling Vicuña

Once out of the doldrums we were really bound for Cape Horn.

At the beginning of our voyage we had carefully rigged life lines—that is, we had stretched ropes along the length of the main deck at a height to be easily reached. For when the ship rolled in heavy seas, when waves broke over her, or the decks were filled with water, sailors could be swept off their feet. By locking their arms over the ropes it was possible to avoid being drowned or washed overboard.

One day, as we neared the Cape, the waves pounding us were dangerously high. The Mate was stationed on the leeside of the poop awaiting orders. He saw that the lee fore braces needed hauling taut and sent the boatswain to call the Watch who were at work under the fo'c'sle head. As the boatswain dashed along the leeside of the main deck, he saw a huge wave mounting high above the weather bulwarks, ready to crash on board. He made a dive for the life line. At the same instant the lift of the wave submerged the lee rail and poured in on deck like a mighty waterfall. The boatswain slipped and missed the life line. He became completely submerged and the streaming water was joined by the wave that had crashed on board over the weather rail. He was afloat and might have been swept into the raging South Atlantic, to be forever lost, but he was carried head-first along the rail. He grabbed the rail and clung. The deck cleared and he struggled to his feet with nothing worse than a bleeding nose and a dislocated elbow.

I took him to my cabin and as I snapped the elbow into place he cried like a child, more from relief at being safe, I imagine, than from pain, for he was a brave young fellow and went back on duty in half an hour.

I had had a similar narrow escape when on the *Erin's Isle* in the same region and I was not unsympathetic. On that occasion had the sea swept out again over the rail, instead of along the deck, I'd have gone with it.

It was off the Horn that I caught my first starfish. We had been dredging and when dumping out the dredge net on the deck, I saw a little starfish with one leg missing. It was a tiny thing. I picked it up by the body and as I did so, off came another leg. This continued until only one was left. The starfish literally throws its limbs at you. In this manner if one is holding it by a limb, the creature succeeds in escaping.

The starfish is found on coral reefs, on sea beaches, and in some parts of the ocean bed. Those found in tropical waters are often of gorgeous colours. When picked up they appear dead but this is only affected. They are of many different sizes but all have one thing in common—the number of limbs equipped with thousands of tiny feet or suckers.

The starfish moves over the bottom of the ocean and in any direction by the use of these little "feet," which although they look soft and frail are strong enough in muscle to open an oyster. When this fish sights an oyster it plants itself over its prey like a small tent, attaches its centre suckers to the upper shell, humps its back and wraps its rays around, sucking below as well. Eventually the oyster gets tired of trying to keep the shell closed. Once the shell is opened the starfish thrusts in his legs and the suckers get to work. In no time at all there is an empty shell. The persistence of the starfish is a quality which mortals could copy to advantage.

In appearance this fish presents an exquisite blending of colour and a mathematical design by means of funny rows of knobs and lumps up and down the rays and on the body.

Starfish are most beautiful when seen on coral sand through

just enough depth of water to give them the faintest tint of azure.

There are many starfish with fancy names, but the most common is the five-fingered species.

The mouth is on the under side with deep grooves radiating to the ends of the fingers. The grooves are really water vessels. The stomach is a single sac with tubes extending into each ray.

The starfish reproduces by means of milt or eggs which leave the fish through pores situated near the body end of each finger.

This creature is a capable athlete. Its supple body by clever gymnastics can squeeze through very small crevices.

It is a scavenger of the sea but also lives on sea food such as clams, mussels, barnacles, and so forth. Perhaps its favourite food is the oyster, and this is a real problem for oyster fishermen. One way in which fishermen meet this threat to their livelihood is by dredging the seaweed in early summer at a period when it contains the starfish young.

Food is taken into the stomach through the same opening as that used for elimination. Sometimes the stomach is turned inside out and wrapped around the fish's prey. After digestion the stomach is drawn in again, leaving the excreta on the outside.

Starfish have enormous appetites. A baby fish less than an inch across has been known to eat 50 clams in six days.

The starfish multiplies rapidly and in large numbers. However, nature takes care of this over-population. The larvae are taken in as food through the gills of other fish, and when more mature the creature is eaten by such birds as gulls and crows.

What amazed me in my study of sea life was the different sizes to be found in the fully grown of a single species.

After we rounded the Cape and began to experience the adventures of sailing in the South Pacific, we took a passenger on board.

We were enjoying a brief spell of fine weather and took advantage of this (and the fact that we were making good time) to do a bit of exploring.

We had just returned from one of these stolen holidays when the Second Mate complained to me of severe abdominal pains. He was feverish and the location of the pain alarmed me. We were closer to the mainland of Peru than to any vessel which might have a doctor on board.

In the gig, I set out with him for the mainland, taking two apprentices with me.

We put in to port at Mollendo. From here a railway company had lines which ran away into the interior across the Andes, through one of the highest passes in the world – 14,666 feet, to the city of La Paz in Bolivia. Before reaching La Paz the railway passed through Arequipa, a city, where a hospital was located. A doctor aboard an American mail boat at Mollendo ordered that my officer should be taken to this hospital. I left the apprentices at the port and went with him for he was a very sick man. He required a delicate kind of operation which the doctor at the port did not feel qualified to perform.

Arequipa is famous for a wonderful volcano, long extinct. Its shape was somewhat similar to the famous Fujiyama in Japan, much larger than Vesuvius, and towering 19,000 feet.

The executives of the railway, who lived in Arequipa, heard of our arrival there. The president and his attractive wife asked me to stay with them which I did for three days until the operation was successfully performed and the Mate able for the return journey to Mollendo. They had one child, a little girl of five years. Someone had given her a baby male vicuña for a pet, which she prized as a sort of pony.

He resembled a young fawn with long slim legs and a silk-like coat of hair. He had been very small when presented to her but grew quickly until he was taller than she. The vicuña was not domesticated. He had ways of defending himself and of showing displeasure which became very embarrassing and sometimes painful.

A paddock had been built for him outside a neat stable. Here he grazed and exercised. If anyone came near, when he was in a bad temper, the vicuña would spit balls of chewed grass with the accuracy of a pea-shooter and to a distance of 10 or 15 feet.

Even his little mistress had suffered from this mean sport. Soon, the vicuña would be full grown and unsuitable for a child's pet. Her father explained that she loved the animal and therefore to have him destroyed was unthinkable. The father had heard that I was fond of animals and a student of natural history. As I had rounded the Cape and the rest of my voyage was unlikely to be stormy, would I take the vicuña to North America and present him to a zoo?

This was something of a challenge to my interest in untamed wild life but I suddenly thought of the four staunchions or posts under the boat skids. They were placed about fifteen feet apart. We could put a fence around them, making a pen. The ship was well loaded but not too heavily. Had the latter been so, the waves would have broken on board and swept the animal away.

The vicuña travelled by rail with us to Mollendo. We left him there in the charge of the railway officials until we returned to the ship. The Mate was now out of danger. After quickly constructing a "cabin" for our strange passenger, we sailed into Mollendo. The vicuña was housed in a railway shed. The Boys, eager and excited, went with me to get him. He recognized me at once and coming to me put his head under my arm. It was an easy matter to slip a rope around his neck. The Boys patted him and fed him biscuits. He came willingly with us.

We let the vicuña loose in the hold of the *Arctic Stream* while we put some finishing touches on his new home. It was dusk when we went to get him. It was dark in the hold. We couldn't see him nor I think, could he see us. Finally we cornered him and with a firm hold around his neck, we frog-marched Mr. Vicuña, hoisted him to the deck and introduced him to his new home. Once inside he took to his heels. Round and round he sped until tired out. Then he lay down on a bed of old canvas which we had arranged for him. But we soon learned that he preferred to lie on hard wood which, no doubt, reminded the poor creature of the firm pampa or soil of its natural home.

In a day or two he acted quite content. We put a pile of dried grass in the pen which he liked to eat but also to spit in partly digested balls at anyone who appeared, with the exception of Allan, a red-haired A.B.

The vicuña and Allan became fast friends. He was the only crew member who was welcome in the pen. Whether he carried food or not, the vicuña came close and nuzzled up to him, waiting to be petted.

Sometimes we let him out on deck for exercise and it was then he showed his dislike for those of the crew who sometimes teased him. Rogers, a stocky Swede, was the worst offender and if he put in an appearance when our pet was out of the pen, the vicuña made for him and if able to come close enough would spit a volley of grass balls into his face.

Sometimes the vicuña would walk quietly around the deck inspecting everything, or run effortlessly the length of the deck, some 180 feet.

"I wish the horses I bet on when we were in Sydney could run like that," the Mate said one day.

The old sailmaker, William, who had often attended the whippet races in Wales said, "If he can run like that, I bet he can jump."

"Let's try him," I said.

One of the fore braces and a quarter inch rope lay slack on the deck stretched part way across.

William picked up the bight of the rope and tightened it a little from the rail. He raised it about two feet off the deck as the vicuña approached.

The animal sailed over about two feet above it.

The next time he came forward, William raised it another

two feet. Again the vicuña jumped it without apparent effort.

William now fastened the rope to the top rail and held the other end on a level with the rail, almost six feet.

Mr. Vicuña now seemed to enter into the spirit of the thing—he all but flew over it.

We were afraid to raise it higher in case he would turn aside and go over the bulwarks into the sea.

The vicuña resumed his stroll as if nothing unusual had happened while the Mate and the sailmaker sat on the hatch making plans as to how they were going to win at the races. Meanwhile, the Swede, who had been taking his two hours at the wheel, was relieved and came forward, strolling nonchalantly along the deck on the port side. From the starboard side, the vicuña spied him and approached. Seeing the expression in the creature's eyes the Swede began to run. The vicuña began to run too, not attempting to overtake him but keeping right behind him, while the Watch below who were sitting along the forecastle head and around the fore bitts shouted encouragement to both.

"Make a touchdown, Swedie," they cried.

But it was not the Swede who made the touchdown. As they neared the forecastle, the vicuña took one of his effortless leaps and with his sharp, protruding teeth, gave his enemy such a dig in the back that he yelled for help, and fell in over the forecastle doorstep. The vicuña stopped, eyed his fallen foe for a moment and then strolled along aft to his pen, where a meal was waiting. On the way he gave a peculiar grin to another crew member whom he did not like, making him reach for the rigging and pull himself out of range. But the vicuña was soon munching his hay, indifferent to the laughter of the watchers.

By the time we reached Oregon, the little girl's pet was almost fully grown with  beautiful reddish brown, soft shaggy wool. The vicuña is related to the alpaca and the llama. From his wool an expensive cloth is made, called vicuña cloth. His home is in an almost rainless region, and therefore he required little to drink.

I had grown attached to the animal and although he preferred Allan to me, sometimes he would allow me to stroke him, standing docile and tame while I did so. But if I made a sudden quick movement, he would leap away.

When we reached Oregon we had difficulty in landing the vicuña because his name did not appear under any classification in the Customs' list. The Customs official called him a sheep. A domestic animal, he said, could not be landed without a permit and how could a permit be granted without a listed name?

Allan had already taken the animal ashore. For this I was severely reprimanded. The fine for doing so without permission would be one thousand dollars. A telephone call to an animal park to which Allan had taken his friend cleared me of guilt. The owner bought the vicuña. We left Oregon satisfied that he had found a good home.

Although he had been born 10,000 feet above the sea on dry and barren plains, he was never seasick on board and when we returned to Oregon a year later we found him healthy and apparently quite happy. He had a decent-sized enclosure, and when he caught sight of Allan and myself, he came leaping. The owner opened the netted gate for us and the vicuña pressed close to us to be petted.

It was our last trip to Oregon and our last visit with the strangest animal I ever took to sea.

# Currents and Curios

The oceans of the world are restless and moody and they are crossed by many currents. Some of these currents are permanent, that is, they exist all the time. Others are temporary and may be brought about by a change in air pressure during a storm, or by some eruption on the sea floor.

When sailing from continent to continent I used to place a paper in a sealed bottle and toss the bottle overboard. On the paper I recorded my name and the name of my ship, also its location, and the date, and requested an answer from the finder. I did this frequently and kept a record for my own use of place and time. Also I numbered the bottles. In all there were over 400 of them. Only a few were returned to me. One bottle which I dropped overboard in the South Atlantic near the coast of Brazil in 1910 was found and returned to me from the East coast of South Africa more than ten years later. Currents had evidently carried it southward around the Cape and then across the great Pacific.

Of course, many of the bottles would be shattered on some rocky shore or in the ocean by powerful ships, but the half dozen which were returned, proved the influence of currents and the extent of their courses.

The Gulf Stream which is often referred to as an ocean river is a current of great importance. It flows for 2,000 miles through the ocean without its waters co-mingling. The temperature of this stream may be many degrees warmer than the body of water through which it passes.

Another strange location of currents is in the Sargasso Sea. This "sea" covers an area of more than two and a half million square miles eastward and northward from the Straits of Florida. Its surface is a mass of floating seaweed, crossed or threaded by rivers.

During the early days of exploring when men believed that the world was flat, navigators who sailed into this region believed that its boundary was the edge of the world.

When I was Captain of the *Arctic Stream* and later of the *Elginshire*, I sailed through the Sargasso Sea many times. Dreadful stories have been told and written of victims swallowed by this sea. I saw the remains of two ship wrecks among the weeds and I admit that it is a weird place, but many of the tales are surely only tales. The area is like a floating island of enormous size, water-soaked, but it is really a shallow platter. Strange creatures live among and under the covering, large and small sea life, but this is not the place of horror which many writers have depicted it to be.

On one occasion we sailed into the Sargasso at dusk and were becalmed there for three days. As we entered by a sort of river, a mass of weed built up against the bow and trailed alongside. Clear water was seen only from the stern, uncovered by the passing of the ship, and this was soon covered again. When night fell, our crew on and off watch gathered on deck. The silence was eerie. The tendency of sailors at leisure to sing songs and crack jokes did not affect us that night. Voices were quieter than usual. Those who had binoculars used them vainly trying to see what might be alive around us. Here and there on the floating foliage a momentary flicker of light suggested the presence of insect life or some rare species of fish.

We had dropped anchor no more than thirty yards from another of the many rivers which threaded the great sea of weeds. Floating debris, black from age, waited with us for a breeze to affect its position. The sky was faintly overcast and no stars were visible, but about ten o'clock a full moon came up making the blackness even blacker. The debris stood out in the shape of a long canoe, resembling those hollowed out in the early ages from the trunks of sturdy trees by men with crude tools, or burned out if tools were not available.

"Could be it floated there from some American Indian village," said the Mate.

"Could be it's not a canoe or never was. Wait till morning. I'll bet it's part of one Columbus lost when he tangled with this seaweed."

"Did he lose a ship here?"

I thought I detected a note of anxiety in the Mate's voice.

I laughed. "If he did, they left that out of the history books I read as a boy," I said. "But it's certainly part of someone's good ship and for him I am sorry. Probably floated into that river after being wrecked far off in a storm or attacked by pirates."

I think none of us slept too well that night. I joined those on watch about midnight because I was so fascinated by the nature of the place, as much by what I couldn't see as by what was visible. Movement among the weeds was audible but not frightening–the stir of small creatures, I thought, disturbed by our presence and not intending to harm us.

Morning might bring some surprises. I would have considered examining that barge-like wreckage but I had no hope of doing so–my gig could not be safely piloted through such a tangle of sea growth and who could say what might be hiding under it?

But daylight did bring surprises for the overcast sky cleared and the sun spread first rose and then golden rays over the sea's surface. By quiet observance during three almost cloudless days I learned many things about the inhabitants of that strange region out of which some seamen had never found their way, and where Columbus is said to have been involved for a fortnight.

We discovered that, contrary to popular opinion, the seaweed was not one great connected mass but divided patches floating so close together that it had the appearance of such connection. A ship entering through one of its streams might come to a sudden blocking of weed (the river's ending it appeared), but if one sailed ahead, the block would yield becoming a clinging fringe alongside, a harmless gathering, slowing the vessel but otherwise doing it no harm.

A Scotsman, Sir John Murray, financed in his explorations by the Norwegian government, reported in 1910 that the weed was not a solid mass and that ships could not become permanently restrained by it. This I know to be true.

In daylight we sighted many small fish among the kelp, some minnow-sized of brilliant colours, and one queer creature which may have explained the appearance of specks of light here and there in the darkness. I caught this specimen by using a butterfly net in a small pool that formed over the seaweed at the lee side of the ship. He was shaped like a child's rubber ball, almost black, with a large mouth and a row of teeth angled inward. A muscled rod-like thing was fastened to his upper lip. This projection had a tiny light at the end. This light may have been given him by nature to aid him in finding food such as larvae and minute insects on the kelp. That he was a night hunter we suspected from the twinkling we had seen among the seaweed. But his prey was not confined to small fry. I received a shock when I examined his stomach. There I found a pinkish coloured fish almost eight inches long. My captive measured only half that length from rod to tail. Obviously I had netted a rare specimen. I found this to be true when I took his skeleton to the British Museum upon my return to England. Up to that time nothing like him had been caught and I was told that his home was more than 10,000 feet down in the ocean. What had brought him to the surface of the Sargasso Sea was a mystery. In the darkness of the ocean depths the tiny lantern which was part of his anatomy was a wonderful asset. I do not know of another deep sea creature provided with such equipment.

Caught in the mess of my butterfly net was another strange

creature of the deep—the corpse-like stone lily. I have never thought the name a suitable one for it does not take note of the strangest of its features. It is a fragile delicate thing, more like a fern in structure with tiny leaf lobes stripped off and just the stems left.

Through millions of years the stone lily has not changed in shape or behaviour so far as we know. The specimen I caught in the Sargasso was dead and had floated up many thousands of feet, in some way becoming detached from the garden—the ocean floor. A longer thicker stem led downward from the branches. I took the skeleton to my cabin where I kept a small but up-to-date library dealing with seafaring and creatures of the sea. I found an illustration of the lily. By the longer, thicker stem it stood attached on the floor of the ocean, its fronds or branches reached upward, like a miniature tree.

Among many other forms of life there we saw a few pipe fishes and a number of small seahorses. The pipe fish may be described as a proud fellow who swims with his nose in the air, this feature being a stem-like projection upward. The pipe fish is slender and quite small, often referred to as a poor relation of the seahorse.

The true seahorse gets its name from its shape, the head and front part of the fish, especially. The tail is long, slender and tapering and has no fins. The fish wears a coat of armour; really a skeleton in segments. It curls up its tail and attaches itself with it to objects such as seaweed. With body erect, its head is that of a tiny horse. The seahorse is happy in the Sargasso for it has only one fin (along its back) and cannot swim rapidly. It finds food by moving easily from place to place among the kelp, refastening itself and almost appearing as part of the vegetation, thus evading its enemies. One has to look closely to distinguish the fellow from his habitation. Some are only two inches long—the longest no more than 12 inches (There is a species in Australian waters that measures 2 feet.) It lives on the small fry of other fishes and on spineless sea food to be found where it lives.

Once in a current this little creature lacks the equipment to escape from it. His one fin is only adequate for movement from object to object.

It seemed a pity to remove such harmless little creatures from the shelter they had found but I did capture two by cutting away pieces of the seaweed on which they were anchored and placing weed and horses in a tub of sea-water. I added clumps of kelp with fish larvae and insect life each day until we were beyond the region but they survived less than a week.

The Sargasso Sea was a fascinating place. Three days passed quickly and I was really sorry when a light breeze changed to a fine westerly wind. Soon we were on our way and able to state from experience that the weed-strewn area was not a place to dread but to explore.

There are many false stories told and retold about parts of the water world. The Sargasso Sea has been treated as a place of horror and the ocean around Cape Horn as one of continuous bad weather and raging storms. The perils of both regions have been over-stressed.

It is true that rounding the Horn is rarely accomplished without encountering stormy seas, but when Master of the *Elginshire*, I was becalmed there. Fine weather is not unusual to the region and on this occasion there was a period of quiet seas under bright sunny skies. We were East of the Horn islands and edging slowly southward when the wind died. We were in water about 400 feet deep and could see fish, large and small, passing us not too far below the surface.

Idling a bit, several of the crew occupied their time fishing. Two fine cod and several smaller fish were landed. It was a suitable spot to try a net and dredge, near as we were to a continental shelf. I rigged up net and dredge and towed them along the bottom. My hope was to capture species that would not take a hook and this happened. When I hauled up after half an hour or so, there were small things inside the net and tangled in the fringe, half plant, half animal in appearance, all very much alive. I recognized some small lime-white starfish, and a tiny thing like a miniature octopus. I picked it out of the collection and it curled itself around my finger. When I tried to uncoil it, I found that although it had seemed flexible, at my touch it stiffened and bits came off in my hand but it was still alive.

The creature was a crinoid. There were several of them, some whole, some in bits, and I recognized their similarity to the fern-like corpse which I had found in the Sargasso.

Encouraged by the findings of our first attempt to dredge in that area, I tired again. This time I attached several hooks along the dredge wire and even as the apparatus was lowered there was a violent wrench. The wire snapped and a thousand feet of it, together with all attached apparatus, was lost.

I coveted the opportunity to explore further around the Horn in the area of the islands where the rocky shelf invites many species of sea life to gather, but the opportunity never came. On other voyages the Horn lived up to its reputation – storm – and storm challenges everyone's attention.

When conditions threatened the safety of our ship we lay to under the lee of the islands. There, it would have been safe enough to fish and dredge but in a howling gale with heavy spray of rain or sleet lashing in on deck, no one cared to expose themselves more than duty required.

# Monkeys as Passengers

We had taken a cargo of lumber from Victoria, B.C., to South Africa. Again the ship was the *Arctic Stream*. Although I had a more experienced crew on this voyage, I retained as well several who had proved themselves capable on the sail to Portland, Oregon.

Allan was still with me, and the African sun touching his red hair gave it a fiery tinge.

Whether animals have a preference for certain colouring in humans, I don't know, but our new passenger, a monkey which we called Diana, immediately attached herself to Allan as had our former animal passenger, the vicuña. Diana possessed a very uncertain temperament and had the bad habit of biting, even in play. This habit had caused her former owner, a shipbroker in the port of East London, a great deal of concern. His small daughter for whom he had bought the pet, had suffered a severe bite on the forefinger. He approached me about accepting the animal as a sort of mascot. What I would decide to do eventually with Diana did not greatly concern him, he said. He believed that her bad temper had developed from teasing by a neighbour's children. She had been kept tied in a fenced yard. These children, knowing that she could not escape from them, had frequently vaulted the fence and amused themselves by pinching her tail. I believe that mean treatment will develop bad temper in almost any animal.

We were in East London for a week and during this time we kept our monkey tethered on deck while we prepared a house for her.

I built the house for Diana to protect her in bad weather from cold winds and lashing seas. The house was about five feet square with two windows and a kennel roof. A removable panel in the door could be replaced by one of screen. A pole in the centre of her home extended from deck floor to roof tip with two crossbars where she could exercise or sit and watch what was going on through windows and the door.

Diana accepted her new home with alacrity. It was a different matter, however, when anyone approached the kennel to feed her or to attach a leading rope to her pretty leather harness. The rope was long enough to give the monkey considerable freedom on deck when made fast to the rail.

Diana appeared to dislike me especially although it was I who fed her and talked to her, hoping that my attentions would eventually win her favour. But whenever I appeared, she showed her teeth. It was a feat to slip a bowl of food or water into her domain without being bitten. As to petting her—I would rather have stroked a man-eating tiger.

There are many species of monkeys. Diana was small, about 3 feet from nose to tail-tip. She was short-haired and dull grey in colour. She wore a cynical expression and had the habit of talking to herself, complaining, one felt, of her captivity.

A week after Diana came aboard we set sail from East London for Port Pirie, Australia. We ran into stormy weather and the temperature dropped considerably. The monkey had to be kept in her house. With the first onset of storms she became very seasick and for a while acted the part of a whimpering docile child. But with the return of fine weather as we approached the port, her bad temper also returned.

I gave up offering my attentions to Diana and turned over her care and feeding to Allan. Whether he approached her house to feed her or to release her for a walking tour sitting on his shoulder, she greeted him with a chatter of delight. She would press her face against his cheek and sometimes ruffle his hair with her front paws or hands.

Her treatment of the rest of the crew remained unfriendly. When she was tethered on deck those going to or coming from their turn at steering would cross to the other side of the deck to avoid passing Diana. She seemed to dislike especially anyone taking the wheel, perhaps because she thought them responsible for the motion of the ship.

One of our crew was a heavily built Norwegian. His hair was a whitish blonde. His skin was fair and he had wide open pale blue eyes. His given name was so hard to pronounce that we called him Ned. Diana acted toward Ned as if he were a stowaway and had no right on board. It was amusing to observe the look of fear on this fellow's face if Diana approached him. Thinking to overcome her dislike of him, I offered Ned the privilege of feeding her. This privilege he politely refused.

One day when Ned was at the wheel Allan strolled along the deck with Diana on his shoulder as usual. Ned was intent upon his job of steering. Without warning Diana made a leap onto Ned's back. With a shout he shook her off and deserted the wheel running forward on the opposite side of the ship. Diana seemed amused by his behaviour. One could have said there was a twinkle in her eye. She did not trouble to follow Ned but climbed upon Allan's shoulder again, and they continued on their way as if nothing had happened.

But something very serious had happened as those who are familiar with ships will realize. To leave the wheel of a ship while it is under way is like a sentry leaving his post or a man in a motor vehicle jumping from it, allowing it to careen unguided, thus endangering the lives of passengers and pedestrians. The sentence for such a man would probably be the absolute limit of the law. To leave a great vessel unguided is an offence fully as serious. Fortunately for us, the water was clear of rocks ahead and the wind was not strong. It was obvious to me that the unexpected attack by Diana had driven an otherwise conscientious crewman to desert his post in fear of being chewed up by a savage monkey. The Mate who was close by had taken the wheel and no harm was done. Neither Ned nor the monkey were chastised by me but I advised Allan not to approach the wheel with his friend again.

On another occasion Diana somehow evaded Allan's watchful eye and was found sitting close to the wheelsman, a dark Italian lad. She showed her teeth in a menacing manner when the Mate and I approached her, ready to take over should she frighten the young Italian as she had Ned. At the sight of us, however, she chattered gleefully, ran across the deck to the rail, jumped onto it and climbed up the rigging. We stayed close by. We knew not what scheme might be forming in Diana's head. Allan, in search of her, was distressed and offered to go aloft after her. I might say that no one else thought of doing this for in her position she could use one pair of hands to cling to the ropes and attack whoever approached with the other pair. While I debated whether Allan should be allowed to go after her, she sat showing her teeth at me. I knew that with her ability to climb she could keep the whole crew chasing her if she sprang from rope to rope.

"I am afraid she will jump into the sea," Allan said. "Let me go up, sir. She's my friend."

The expression in Allan's eyes affected me greatly. "Don't worry," I comforted him, "She is too smart to risk being drowned. Hunger will bring her down."

Even as I said it I realized that this might mean a long period of watching and waiting too – a night and day watch which would keep the crew on edge. And if a severe storm came up, what then?

I turned to Allan. "You have my permission to bring her down," I said, "if you can do it, but I hope you realize that you are attempting this at your own risk."

Allan did not hesitate and as he went up the mizzen rigging, Diana, with gleeful chatter, ran before him up to the topmost yard, the Royal yard; and there, 120 feet above the deck, she waited. As he neared her, she crossed from the Royal mast to the main mast, and up again. It would now be necessary for Allan to come down and go up the main mast. This was quite an undertaking but Allan was determined. He slid rapidly down the backstays, dashed to the main mast and up he went. We were watching for Diana's next move but she sat still, looking far out to sea. As Allan reached for the foot rope on the Royal yard, Diana saw him and leaped skilfully, landing on his shoulder. When Allan reached the deck Diana's arms were around his neck and she remained in that position as he carried her to the kennel.

The friendship between Allan and the monkey was even stronger after this exciting episode. Indeed it was beginning to have an effect on Diana's general disposition. Up to this time it had been Diana's habit when anyone else came in view to show her distaste of them by screaming, while her expression revealed positive hate. Now she often chattered pleasantly to herself and the sinister look gave place to a smile of welcome. For the rest of the voyage one might say that Diana was a well-mannered passenger.

When we approached Port Pirie we learned from a pilot who came on board that the Australian law prohibited the landing of a monkey. This was a fine kettle of fish. He also said that if we did not land Diana and should she escape from the ship by herself we would be fined $500 whether or not the escape was accidental. There was nothing for it but to keep a good watch on Diana and this was done. It was like having a ship on board a ship—the watch was changed every four hours during the period of my absence on shore. All was well when I returned at dusk. My first question was, "How is the monkey?" They said she had been very quiet all day. They had not ventured to take her from the kennel.

We discharged cargo and reloaded the next day. Before we set sail a young lad, son of the skipper of another vessel about to leave for South Africa, came aboard with his father to see Diana. Since her behaviour when Allan was present would be more polite, I thought, I requested Allan to escort the visitors.

I went about my duties and was talking to the helmsman when I realized that someone was standing at my elbow.

It was Allan, open-mouthed and obviously upset. Diana was gone, he said. She had broken through the netting of the door panel. For a moment I found it impossible to express my feelings. I saw myself in jail or short of $500.

"I'll work it out, sir," Allan said, "if we can't find her. But please, sir, will you delay sailing until we make a search?"

The visiting captain and his boy supported Allan in his plea. I yielded. Even as we talked I became aware that the awning under which we were standing was being shaken. The day was calm and I was puzzled. Relief and chagrin co-mingled as I caught sight of Diana peering over the edge of the awning and grinning gleefully. Like a flash she was up the rigging.

On the look for her, Allan had left us. There was a shout for him and he came on the run out of the half-deck. He started up after the monkey and she led him a merry chase. Then from the Royal yard she turned suddenly and sprang into his arms. By the time he reached the deck, most of those on board had gathered round. "We can't go on like this," I said to Allan, as Diana smiled from his shoulder. "She is too troublesome. The risk is too great." The look he gave me was pathetic.

The captain's son had red hair! Diana, even as she clung to Allan, was smiling at the boy. Would this be the answer to our problem? What was my amazement when the monkey leaped lightly from Allan's shoulder onto that of the young visitor. With one arm around his neck, Diana smoothed his hair with her hand.

"I want her for my pet," the boy was appealing to his father now. Diana had claimed him. Allan looked sorrowfully after the small boat which carried Diana with her new owner to another ship but I think in his heart he was glad. Had she remained with us she might have met an unhappy fate.

About a year later, we took a cargo of coal from Cardiff, Wales, to Brazil. We dropped anchor in the port of Santos.

The coal was for the famous São Paulo Railway. As early as 1906 Brazil had over 10,000 miles of railway, and coal was an important import.

In Santos I found a dealer in monkeys as pets and I told him the story of Diana. He spoke Spanish better than English but he made clear to me that had Diana still been with us he would have purchased her gladly. She was, as he said, an unusual personality.

Francisco was an unusual personality himself. He was a small, thin man, dark of course, with clear steady black eyes. His eyes had a mesmeric quality and held one attentive as he talked. He explained that he had never married and did not care for children. He preferred a family of monkeys. When he parted with one by sale he said it pained him. When he lost one by death, he mourned. It was his nature to prefer animals to human beings, he explained, although human beings were only over-civilized animals, deprived creatures by their own conceit.

Beyond his shop and stretching towards the sea, was an acre or more of sandy ground with a plentiful growth of trees. The plot was fenced above and on all sides. This was a playground for his pets.

He had monkeys of many species but most of them were smaller than Diana. They behaved as one big happy family. One knew that they were not living in fear and that they were well cared for. Francisco had a half dozen marmosets and I bought two from him. He gave me my choice and I noticed how affectionately he fondled them as he placed them in a large box with a netted lid. He gave me detailed instructions on how to care for them.

Marmosets are of the monkey family but very small, not quite as big as a squirrel. They have very long somewhat bushy tails and queer little bewhiskered and wrinkled faces. Their colour is brown.

I regret to say that my new pets were very frightened of me at first. I made a sort of felt harness for them and secured them in a spare room beside my cabin. They chattered nervously to each other and found it difficult, I could see, to accept a change of ownership and environment.

We were sailing the next morning and therefore I had considerable business to attend to. Aside from feeding and watering the small creatures, I left them to themselves for a couple of days, but when in my cabin I could hear them jumping up and down and chattering unhappily. This troubled me. I had bought them especially to make a study of their species but I began to wish that I had left them in their happy home.

However, after we set sail and I had more leisure to consider them, they became calm and very friendly. When I had my cup of tea in the cabin, they would climb up on the tea table, each with a biscuit, and would happily keep me company. I offered them tea in a saucer and they seemed to enjoy it, one on each side, nibbling their biscuits between sips. After they grew more accustomed to me they would finally hop up on my shoulder, one on either side, and curl their long tails around my neck.

I had a soft rubber ball which I used to toss to them when their harness had been removed and they had the freedom of the cabin. Their manoeuvres with the ball revealed part of their nature. Neither would take the ball away from the other. Instead they would share it one with the other.

Although male and female, they did not breed, but they were nevertheless a devoted, loving pair. I placed a warm blanket on the floor in the corner of their room and they lay touching each other, sometimes with front paws interlocked in sleep. When we sailed in cold regions I fluffed up the blanket so they could cuddle into its folds.

Allan left the marmosets to me. He had not gotten over the loss of Diana, I think. He became moody and on our return to England announced to me that he was through with sailing and intended to marry and settle down on land. That was the last I saw of Allan.

Before leaving port again, I gave my pets to the wife of a

prominent doctor in Liverpool. Seafaring had its perils for them and I did not wish to see them suffer, perhaps die.

Marmosets were, for some time, a great society pet. Ladies carried them around in their muffs or perched on their shoulders. I think there is no more affectionate, gentle creature. If properly fed and protected from the cold, they will live for a long time.

Some countries prohibit their importation because of their susceptibility to pneumonia, believing them to be carriers of the germ as well as easy victims of the disease.

I missed my little friends very much, but when our next voyage proved to be an exceptionally rough and dangerous one, I was glad I had left them behind.

# Jennie and the White Kitten

The boat was the *Elginshire* and I was Captain. We were on our way home from Manila to New York.

A short distance out from port we sighted a piece of floating wreckage, certainly broken from the wooden rail of a ship. We had heard while in port that only a few days before our arrival a tug and a pilot boat had collided during a storm and that the pilot boat had been damaged. The pilot boat had lost most of her gear and was in dock for repairs.

The sun had set. The wreckage against the rich after-glow was black. On the black was a spot of white.

"It's moving," Wilson, the Mate said to me. "That thing's alive."

"A rat, maybe," I answered, but I kept my eye on it as we sailed closer.

"Lower the boat," I ordered two of the apprentices, "and find what's there and bring it in."

They obeyed me eagerly and in half an hour returned with the prettiest white kitten I have ever seen. Its belly was dripping wet but the back of it was dry and showed a beautiful coating of hair.

The poor thing was weak from starvation and had given itself up willingly. Soon it was lapping milk from a tin plate. When it had finished, the boys gently dried it off.

"Take it to my cabin," I said. "As soon as I can I'll see to it. With your permission it will be the skipper's cat."

They laughed. They knew my fondness for animals.

"I'll put it in the room next to mine," I added, "when it gets over its fright."

"What about Jennie, sir?" one of the apprentices asked.

For the moment I had forgotten Jennie. "I'll take care of that," I said crisply—crisply but with secret misgivings.

Appreciating my interest in monkeys, the stevedore had given me a pair while we were in Manila. The room next to mine was occupied by Jennie. Jock, the male, had died two days after they were taken on board, from eating cockroaches. The latter were plentiful on wooden ships and Jock's appetite for the crunchy, indigestible pests was enormous, with fatal results. The body of a cockroach is not like that of a grasshopper or caterpillar. Such insects are part of a monkey's diet and have some food value. But the cockroach seems to have none.

Deprived of her mate, Jennie depended more and more on the crew for friendship and became very tame. She scorned cockroaches, to her good fortune, and was a well-behaved passenger. But how would she accept a new room-mate? We were to experience a surprise.

Jennie not only approved of the kitten but often cradled it in her arms. Soon they were given the freedom of the ship and their games of "catch who catch can" and competition for the friendship of the cook kept the crew in good spirits. We had quite a spell of fair weather too, which encouraged contentment.

But with the passing of time, Snowball, as we called the kitten, lost interest in lullabies. She danced and purred her way into everyone's heart, everyone's but Jennie's. Jealousy began to creep in and whenever Snowball found Jennie beside me or the Mate, she showed her pretty but sharp teeth and nipped the monkey's tail. Then she would dance off while the monkey went to someone whimpering for sympathy.

I now took the kitten into my cabin and left the adjoining room to Jennie. At first I alternated the favour but Jennie had become very mischievous. She had also become very jealous.

It was the custom for both pets to sleep on my bunk at night. Snowball was content to curl herself at my feet but not Jennie. Jennie chose to stretch herself across my chest and often when I woke, her head was tucked under my chin and one of her arms was around my neck. I did not appreciate her expression of affection but one cannot hurt the feelings of a lonely monkey. For Jennie was lonely despite her kitten playmate and no doubt rebellious. And her behaviour became mischievous. If left alone in my room I would find it in disorder—my precious white bedspread on the floor, articles on my dresser in a jumble, and such things as boots and slippers drawn out of the closet and revealing by their position that Jennie had been having a solitary game of ball.

One afternoon when I came down to spend my 4 to 6 Dog Watch reading or studying, Jennie was sitting in the middle of the bed with a smug expression on her wrinkled face. The bedspread was decorated with red foot prints up and down and across. The bottle of red ink on my desk was lying on its side and a pool of red was on the floor.

This was not all. The room looked as if it had been struck by a tornado: under my bunk were lockers filled with various articles needed for the voyage and so kept under my control, among them several gross of small boxes containing matches. I had now a fine chance to count them as every box was out and opened. The matches were piled inches deep on the floor.

When I turned to find Jennie she was nowhere to be seen. I had neglected to close the door. After two hours of tidying up the mess I went up on deck in search of the culprit, but I could not find her. I returned to my cabin. There was a noticeable hump under the cover of my bunk. There was Jennie in hiding.

I seized her by the neck and gave her a good shake and a long lecture in language she seemed to understand. She gave a few monkey moans and coiled up on the foot of the bunk. She lay there with one eye open and when I retired, she did not venture to offer me her usual expression of affection.

Soon after I made a house for Jennie, much like a kennel but larger, with a window and a door screened over. I furnished Jennie's house with a small wooden bunk and coverings to which she was accustomed.

When the ship was in fine weather regions, the house stood on deck with the door open. Jennie was tethered to it by a long rope as a dog to a kennel.

Snowball now became my sole companion in the cabin except during rough weather. Jennie became insanely jealous of Snowball, realizing that the kitten had special privileges.

Whenever we showed Snowball any attention, Jennie would mope or scream as the spirit moved her.

We took on another cat before the end of that voyage, as black as Snowball was white. Ebony gave us two kittens as black as herself before we reached New York. She and her family were steerage passengers—Snowball remained first-class.

One day, when Jennie was not tied, she was sitting on top of her house sunning herself half asleep, with her long tail hanging down a few inches from the deck floor. Along came Snowball in a playful mood. Her tiny white teeth nipped the end of that tail. With a leap and a scream Jennie was after her. Snowball did her best to outdistance the monkey but after two rounds of the deck, made a leap for the rail. Jennie sprang also and gave the kitten a push and it was overboard. As the ship was speeding along in fine Trade Winds the kitten disappeared almost instantly in the boiling water of the ship's wake.

Jennie dashed for her house and locked herself in. It was no use to punish her. That would not bring back our pretty Snowball and who were we to judge the working of a monkey's mind.

Not long after this the crew were cleaning and painting the ship. Out of curiosity Jennie sampled the white lead paint being used. Finding it nice and sweet to the taste she had a few more mouthfuls—with fatal results. We buried Jennie in the same ocean that had swallowed the kitten a few days before.

# An Accident and a Stowaway

We were sailing up the East Coast of South America. It was late summer. I spotted a large cruiser and a cargo boat.

"They aren't on a trade route," I said to the Mate, "and I'm curious."

The cruiser was coming toward us. I put up our ensign and she greeted it with the ensign of Spain. But when I looked at her through the telescope as she turned direction, I examined with some shock the coat-of-arms on her stern. It was German. At dusk the cargo boat flashed a message to the cruiser in the Morse Code and I made out one word, "War."

A few hours later the cruiser came close and turned her searchlight on us. Because we were moving toward Brazil I imagine she believed that was our destination. I kept on to deceive her for a couple of hours and then made straight for St. Helena. It was August 5th, 1914. At St. Helena I learned that Germany and Great Britain were at war.

Soon no allied ships were safe anywhere on the seas. There were submarines in the sea-lanes and mines were laid wherever ships in the service of Great Britain and her allies were likely to go.

The *Elginshire* was soon daring the enemy as were all other allied vessels. To and from she went wherever needed – transporting wheat, petroleum, and whatever she could for the use of our troops, and to feed the people of the British Isles where enemy ships watched every port–finally succeeding in running a blockade which threatened the lives of the population and the assembled troops. We crossed and re-crossed the Atlantic many times. And often it was difficult to maintain our course, as we dodged the enemy, going by irregular and perilous routes.

The end of the War, or shortly after, brought an end to the career of the noble *Elginshire*, but not before we had experienced many adventures and the great privilege of sharing in an allied victory.

We had carried a cargo of oil from Philadelphia to Korea and had returned without cargo to Vancouver where we were loading wheat for Liverpool.

I had a fine crew that season, men willing to risk their lives for their country. The colonies at that time were not only willing but eager to share in the struggle. Three-quarters of my men were of English, Irish and Scottish parentage, with two Frenchmen, an American negro, and an Italian cook in the galley. Most of them were over conscription age and at that time Canadian troops were volunteers only.

Berkeley, one of my Ordinary Seamen, had fallen ill with a serious type of intestinal fever the day before we reached Vancouver. Fearing typhoid, I had him removed at once to the hospital for observation. It was not the dread disease, which would have kept us in quarantine, but a non-contagious stomach ailment. However, when the *Elginshire* had taken on her cargo of golden grain, Berkeley was still weak and though eager to sail with us I thought it wiser to leave him on shore until our next voyage which, if all went well, we expected to make as soon as we could return.

A young Japanese, with two years sailing experience on a freighter which had been badly damaged during a monsoon in the China sea, had become known to me. We engaged in conversation over dinner in a café while we were in port. He was an intelligent well-spoken fellow, Canadian born. He had applied for enlistment in the Canadian Army but had been rejected.

"Why?" I asked.

He smiled. "We are not liked here," he said.

"But you're Canadian."

Again he smiled. "My face is Japanese," he reminded me. "Canada, especially British Columbia, would like to stay white."

"Come to think of it," I mused, "I haven't seen a negro in this town—but yes, there are two now on the gangway of that ship." The café was near the docks. An American ship was loading lumber.

"Yes, I've talked to them," he said. "A cook and a deck hand. You don't see black men, perhaps, in Vancouver, but plenty of us Orientals, Chinese and Japanese. We like Canada but, no, Canada doesn't like us."

I saw the way people looked at us as they came and went in the café. He was right. But the Japanese were our allies. Out there, so I had heard, two Japanese warships had been sent to help guard our coastline from German invasion.

It didn't make sense.

"Men on ships these days are risking their lives for the love of their country as surely as soldiers on land or airmen are. If you mean what you say—if you want to help—come with me. I need a man who has guts and patriotism. Usually the crew of a sailing ship is made up of many nationalities. We're too busy fighting the gales and the hurricanes to lose time spitting at each other."

Junso Mitsuma sailed in the *Elginshire* for the duration of the War. He was a full-fledged A.B. when he left me to join other young Japanese rejected by Canada as aliens, as a student of medicine at a Tokyo University. He would distinguish himself, I felt sure.

However, as the War went on, prejudice lost some of its teeth and a number of Canadian-Japanese were welcomed by the army and navy too. They proved themselves to be good fighters, courageous, and loyal. They received praise and won distinction, but when the war ended "white" Canadians returned to their former habit of biting at oriental heels, especially in British Columbia.

But I shall never forget an episode aboard the *Elginshire* involving Junso as we dodged the enemy on a voyage. This endeared my Japanese crew member to me.

We were heading for Durban, South Africa, when we were overtaken by a cyclonic storm in the Mozambique Channel. It struck us so suddenly that there was hardly time (or need) to shout "All hands." After a hard tussle the *Elginshire* limped her way toward port.

Our First Mate was thrown to the deck during the terrific wind after tripping over a coil of rope and his abdomen came in contact with a corner of the hatch. A serious injury was evidenced by acute pain and the inability to rise even with aid.

Junso found him and came for me. We slipped a wide piece of canvas beneath him to form a four-cornered sling and carried him to my cabin. He was a thickly set man and it took four of us to do this. I watched with admiration while Junso superintended the removal of his wet clothing. He covered him with woollen blankets. While I examined the moaning victim of the storm, Junso brought a warm drink from the galley. "Cocoa—no rum," he said very low. "There may be internal bleeding."

Compassion had caused him to ignore who gives orders on board any ship.

I nodded and went on with my examination.

I slept in the Mate's quarters that night while Junso took over the nursing duties.

About 2 a.m. he tiptoed into my room without knocking. I wasn't asleep and I had a lamp burning.

"He's asleep, sir. The pain is better," he said, "and his colour is better. I think he'll make it, sir."

"In a few hours, I hope, we'll dock," I told him. "Let me relieve you. He can't be left alone."

"No, please, sir. I'm not tired. You'll be needed on deck soon for orders. Do get some sleep, sir. I won't leave him."

He was true to his word. In the morning we sighted our destination. Durban had become a naval base and I was eager to get in for two reasons–the Mate's serious condition and because I had heard there were German submarines in those waters. I signalled for a pilot but none came. I was rather desperate by this time. My ship was drifting. If she passed the port it would take days, perhaps weeks to get her back into position. We had reduced sail but there was a lively wind. I did not delay. I gave orders to move in unattended, with signals from shore ordering me to stop. As we neared the shore, a tug came out. We were about half a mile from shore now. With the tug astern we furled remaining sails and dropped anchor. Without a pilot the *Elginshire* made a neat entrance through a channel known to be dangerous, where even steamers were required to have a pilot on board. But I had risked disobedience, perhaps severe penalty rather than the life of a man I knew to be seriously injured.

Apparently the *Elginshire* was suspected of being a camouflaged German cruiser. When our true identity was confirmed, I was allowed to proceed with caring for the Mate. In the hospital they found that he stood a good chance of recovery but would not be able to leave with us. He would be sent to his home in Liverpool as soon as he was fit to travel.

Then came the settling of my own affairs.

Rumour had it that I was to face a court martial for disobeying naval orders. But a great man was to intercede for me – Commodore Dow of the Cunard fleet who happened to be in Durban at that time on his way to Arabia with troops. He openly defended me and privately praised me. His influence was tremendous with the naval authorities.

This first meeting was the beginning of a lasting friendship. Commodore Dow's home was in England, not far from Liverpool, and I enjoyed many visits with him there.

I introduced Junso Mitsuma to the Commodore while we were at Durban and they had several talks about the problems of Japanese immigrants in America.

"People who treat Orientals as inferiors," Danny Dow said to me, "will one day bow to them as to superiors. Their time will come."

Junso, a capable A.B., was still with me when I took the *Elginshire* to Liverpool on my last voyage as skipper of a sailing ship. There he signed on an American troopship carrying home wounded men fit for the voyage.

But between us Junso and I had been guilty of an unlawful act which may have been excusable in time of war, the conditions of seafaring being what they were.

On leaving a Canadian port with a cargo of food supplies for delivery to a British port, we took on cargo during a drenching rain, common to the West Coast of Canada in the fall and winter seasons.

We had protected the life boats with coverings of canvas and were a considerable distance from land before the storm ceased. Then Junso with an apprentice went to remove the canvases and see that all was well with the boats.

In one of them, somewhat breathless, no doubt, but alive, was the only stowaway I harboured in all my years at sea.

Under conditions of war it would have been folly to turn back, risking our lives and our cargo.

The slim middle-aged man wore cotton shorts and a brown cotton shirt. His feet were bare. His skin was sallow, his eyes and longish hair were dark–the expression of the eyes when I first looked into them was an expression of terror.

Junso had led me to him where he sat cross-legged on the deck by the boats.

"Can you speak English?" I asked him.

He nodded.

"Then tell me who you are and why you came aboard without permission."

He didn't answer.

"You're a conscientious objector I suppose, trying to escape conscription."

He shook his head.

The Japanese spoke up. "Sir, I think he's a Sikh. There are a lot of them in B.C. They aren't wanted either. They're British subjects and can't be kept out legally, they say, but things are getting pretty tough for them."

"Is that what you are? A Sikh?"

He nodded and put his head in his hands. His shoulders shook with emotion.

"Why are you going to England? That's where we're going, I hope, if the Germans don't get us on the way. Your home is India."

He lifted his head. Tears were streaming down his thin brown face. "I have wife and big boy," he said with a queer accent. "I send for them three times–Canada say stay out; you go to England. Live there. England British country. I am British subject. Two my brothers fight for British in war. England let me have my family, or I go home."

I mused. "This country is British, too," I reminded him and myself. "*British* Columbia. What makes you think that the people in England will treat you differently?"

He dropped his head into his hands again but said firmly, "I know. My brothers fight for them."

"For us, too," I thought but did not say.

"Do you want to work for me?" I asked him.

He raised his head and his expression was pitifully eager.

"I work anything," he said. "I work hard. I am not hungry man." He drew two loaves of dry looking bread from a paper bag. I felt my heart soften.

"We can't go back," I said to Junso. "Get him a mug of cocoa and some meat from the galley, and tell the Mate I want to speak to him. I'll have some explaining to do when we get to Liverpool, of course, but as our friend says, 'They treat me good.' "

Junso looked at me as as if I had pardoned his brother.

"I knew you would be kind, sir," he said, and hurried to the galley.

The officials in England were too grateful for the safe arrival

182

of the *Elginshire* with food for hungry mouths to worry about the arrival of one homesick Indian. A vessel was preparing to sail for Bombay. Arnot, as he called himself, signed on as a deck hand, with no questions asked.

"I hope he finds them," Junso said as the vessel with a cargo of coal left port.

"Who?" asked our Second Mate. Junso looked at me. "The people he wants to find," he said.

We had grown to like our dark-skinned helper in the galley, and wished him well.

# *I Could Go on Forever*

Life of the air,
Life of the sea,
You captivate
The heart of me.
Above the waters
And below,
You travel with us
As we go.

When I reflect upon the happenings during my long life of seafaring, I acknowledge that more remains to tell than has been told.

The moods of water and sky in times of calm and of storm never lose their fascination and although shipwrecks are sometimes sighted, presenting a vision of horror, it is astonishing how rarely one sees wreckage when one considers the number of vessels that brave the deep in all weathers.

Mysteries there have been—ships found afloat or shattered on rock-strewn shores, some intact, as if abandoned without reason, not a soul on board nor a clue to explain the cause. Such was the *Mary Celeste*, life boats and other boats waiting in the davits, and a half-eaten meal on the table; treasure untouched in the hold and no explanation for a woman's shoe lying on the deck. The fate of the crew and of the passengers has never been fathomed to this day.

Another tragedy destroyed a ship whose sole survivors were two crew members and the captain and his wife.

The ship was an iron barque of about 900-ton register. She left New York for Rouen, France, carrying a cargo of naphtha in wooden barrels. I knew a member of her crew who asked me, if I told the story of her fate, to withhold her name. With the respect which one seaman has for another no longer alive, I shall call her the *Southern Cross*.

A daughter of the Captain attended a girl's school in Liverpool. She was to meet her parents when the ship docked in France. Two days before the arrival was anticipated, the girl received a wire from Lloyd's which read as follows:

"LIZZARD 9 A.M.

BARQUE SOUTHERN CROSS PASSED FOR ROUEN, ALL WELL."

The time of arrival was estimated and the girl left for Rouen where she lodged with family friends in a chateau not far inland. When two days passed with no news, an inquiry was made at the Pilot Station. She was urged not to feel alarm because there was an east wind and the station believed that it might be two or three days longer before they would hear from the ship owing to the weather conditions.

The east wind ceased and two days later the *Southern Cross* called for a pilot and tug. She had passed Le Havre in tow at six a.m. She would dock at Rouen about five o'clock that afternoon, but the cargo of naphtha would be discharged before anyone left her to go ashore.

The girl found a small café near the wharf and waited. About noon she saw the tip of a ship's mast on the horizon. That was surely the *Southern Cross*. The café owner joined her on a bench overlooking the river. He had a pair of spy glasses and they spent their time waiting and watching for more and more of the mast to appear.

But the tragic fate of the *Southern Cross* made headlines in the Rouen newspaper that night. "BLOWN UP IN THE SEINE ALL BELIEVED LOST." The disaster as reported by the Shipping

Exchange expressed the belief that there were only two survivors—the Mate and the man at the wheel, both of whom had been picked up far astern.

Because of the nature of the cargo neither tobacco nor matches had been issued to the crew during the passage. There had been dissension and discontent. Finally someone had taken a liberty which had caused the deaths of many.

Before the explosion had occurred, the sails had all been furled and the men, off duty, were breakfasting below. The captain and his lady were in their stateroom dressing to land. There was a slight fog and the Mate and the helmsman were on the poop watching for the tug boat from aft.

At the smell of smoke the captain and his wife managed to reach the deck before the boards of the deck floor were ripped open and thrown into the air. Flames and belching smoke followed the explosion and the *Southern Cross* was no more.

But a miraculous rescue took place. Tossed high and beyond the flames into the surging water, the captain held his wife's head above sea level and swam with her to the rudder. The fire crackled around them but the ship was no longer moving ahead and, clinging to the rudder chains, they drifted with the burning hull shoreward. When the hull touched land, they threw themselves onto the river bank and climbing on their hands and knees managed to escape drowning.

Like drenched rats they lay waiting for sufficient breath to reach a hedge of small shrubs which grew up the bank a little farther. The place seemed deserted, and in security behind the hedge they removed their soaking clothing and wrung it as nearly dry as possible. They redressed themselves. The wind was brisk but warm. They were twenty miles from Rouen. They set out on foot, for who would give room in coach or carriage to such dishevelled creatures and without money to pay their way? After several rejections, they sat down to rest. Suddenly the captain's wife cried, "My sovereign."

Around her neck on a chain was a souvenir of the Golden Jubilee which she had worn for years as a lucky piece. She wept with relief, and soon, by payment for their transportation with the solid gold piece, they were rolling away toward Rouen. And when the driver of the coach learned their identity at the end of the journey, the sovereign was returned to its owner. Today it is proudly worn by a grand-daughter in memory of a brave ancestor.

What stories might be told if the sea were to give up her dead. I met the lone survivor of another shipwreck in a coastal village of Ireland. She was known as *The Woman Who Never Smiled*. During a furious storm in the Irish Channel her parents' barquentine was lost with all presumed on board. Then but a child of five, she was rescued from the leaping waters by a fisherman who put out in a small boat to save her at the risk of his own life. She was unconscious.

Later her benefactors tried to learn from her the name of her parents and of the sunken ship. She had lost, it seemed, the memory of everything but the horror of the disaster. Or was it that her lips remained sealed from sorrow? She was brought up in the family of her rescuer and kindly treated, but she never smiled and rarely looked toward the sea. At night she slept with her head covered from the sound of the waves.

When I made the acquaintance of this strange sad girl, she was a worker in the fields with other peasant women. She was the prettiest young woman I have ever seen despite her look of sorrow.

An Irish priest told me her story. She was a gentle soul, he said, and animals loved her. Men desired her but she never married. She came to mass regularly but never to confession.

The last time I visited the village I asked again about this woman who seemed to have vanished. In fact she had fallen backwards off a loaded hay cart and had been fatally injured.

"She did smile once," the priest said, "In death."

It was in the South Seas when exploring a palm-girt small and deserted island that I came upon the remains of another shipwreck. A collar of sand lay around the island but behind the waving palms was perhaps an acre of land, somewhat elevated and with low scrub foliage. I was alone that day. As I set into the place to have a look around, I caught my foot in what I thought was the protruding root of a tree. It proved to be the bone-dry and bare hip bone of a man. I went back to the gig for a shovel.

Carefully and slowly I cleared the ground and then, with the shovel began the excavation. Bits of cloth rotted beyond recognition came away with the earth. I searched for anything which might provide the clue to identity. There was nothing. The body's position suggested an attempt to flatten oneself from the force of a hurricane but again perhaps tossed that way by a raging sea. Scraps of boot leather, I believed, were English.

I laid the skeleton into place as respectfully as I could. This had been a man but flesh and blood and clothing had been turned into dust. There was nothing to be done for him now except to wrap the bones in a ship's blanket and bury them in their former location. I carved a marker, without name or date, from a piece of driftwood, and undertook the grim business of reburial.

I was about to begin the shovelling when my eye caught the outline of something unlike rock or wood. It had been moved from under the corpse by the additional removal of earth to deepen the grave.

I brushed off a thickness of rust and dirt from a flat metal case, not more than an inch and a half square. It was not hinged and when I tried to open it the cover did not yield at the seam but broke into a dozen scraps and fell inward. I took a handkerchief from my pocket and turned out the contents into it.

There lay a piece of red velvet in the form of a tiny envelope, undamaged by time. I lifted the flap with reverence. I knew what it contained because I felt a hard circle within the velvet.

The ring was a band of chased gold such as a man wore in earlier days on his forefinger. Further proof of the mariner's nationality were the few words delicately inscribed inside the band—"Forever with thee," and a heart-shaped symbol.

I waited until after sunset before leaving the island. My thoughts were many. As I sailed away I looked back at the outline of the smallest area of land I had ever visited.

The moon was rising. Did I imagine the crying of a woman in the evening wind, the fluttering of a white figure among the palm trees?

When I returned to England, World War I was at its height. I desired to discover the identity of the only occupant of a lonely island, but the ring, deposited with the shipping fraternity, was never claimed.

The days of sailing ships on the High Seas are past. But as long as the world stands, men will lose their lives in the search for adventure. I think that any true seaman would prefer to rest forever in some remote spot within sound of the waves, rather than to occupy, in conformity with custom, a measured space inland.

> *There is a pleasure in the pathless woods,
> There is a rapture on the lonely shore,
> There is society, where none intrudes,
> By the deep Sea, and music in its roar:
> I love not Man the less, but Nature more.

* Lines from Byron's "Childe Harold's Pilgrimage."

Jessie L. Beattie is the popular author of a dozen books including *Strength for the Bridge* and *A Season Past*. Her work has been read on CBC's *Trans-Canada Matinee*.

Born on an Ontario farm, Miss Beattie wrote and produced a three-act play at the age of fifteen. That same year she won her first prize for poetry. When her first novel appeared, it was greeted with critical acclaim, and reviewers have noted her skill in writing with "an art that conceals art."

Some years ago Jessie Beattie became captivated with Captain Dixon's adventures and she spent long hours with the famous seaman. He shared with her his "log"; and from this diary and the stories he told her, she has woven a memorable account of a great seafarer.